THE GCSE: AN EXAMINATION

THE GCSE: AN EXAMINATION

Edited by
Joanna North

Published by The Claridge Press, 8 Victoria
Square, London, in Association with the
Education Research Trust

First published in 1987
by Claridge Ltd,
8 Victoria Square,
London SW1

© The Claridge Press

Photoset by
Wordsmiths Typesetting Ltd, London N1
and printed by
Short Run Press Ltd, Exeter, Devon

ISBN (paperback edition) 1-870626-10-9
ISBN (clothbound edition) 1-870626-15-X

North, Joanna (edited)
The G.C.S.E.: An Examination

1. Education

CONTENTS

PART ONE

PART TWO

NOTES ON CONTRIBUTORS

COLIN COLDMAN and **KEN SHEPHERD** are both graduates of the Polytechnic of North London, and they both teach Mathematics in ILEA schools.

DAVID COOPER is professor of Philosophy at the University of Durham. His several books include *Illusions of Equality* and *Metaphor*.

NICHOLAS DEBENHAM has been Headmaster of St James Independent School of Boys, since it was founded in 1975.

STEWART DEUCHAR was educated at Repton and Cambridge where he took a degree in History. He has taught History in a private school and, together with his wife, helps on a voluntary basis at an ESN school. He is also Vice Chairman of the Campaign for Real Education.

GISELA M'CAW graduated as a mature student at York University and then took a Diploma in Education. For many years she has taught German at Haberdashers' Monmouth School for Girls where she is Head of the German Department. She wishes to express her indebtedness to Professor Eric Hawkins and Peter Green at the Language Teaching Centre in York.

JOANNA NORTH graduated from Middlesex Polytechnic and then studied Philosophy at Birkbeck College, University of London, where she obtained an MPhil. Her publications include 'Wrongdoing and Forgiveness', *Philosophy* (forthcoming), 'The Politics of Gender' *The Salisbury Review*, Vol. 6, No. 1, and an article on Spinoza in *The*

Oxford Companion to the Mind (forthcoming). She is currently writing a book on Max Scheler.

ANTHONY O'HEAR is Professor of Philosophy at Bradford University. He is the author of numerous books and articles including *Karl Popper*, *Education, Society and Human Nature*, *Experience, Explanation and Faith* and *What Philosophy Is*.

HYWEL WILLIAMS is a master at Rugby School.

JONATHAN WORTHEN is a graduate of Jesus College, Oxford. He has taught in a comprehensive school for a number of years and is currently teaching English at Reigate Grammar School.

SIMON WYATT was educated at Charterhouse, the Royal College of Music and Oxford. He was Assistant Director of Music at Wrekin College, Shropshire for some years and is now Director of Music at Kimbolton School, near Huntingdon.

EDITOR'S ACKNOWLEDGEMENTS

I am grateful to the Centre for Policy Studies for permission to reproduce Stewart Deuchar's essay on GCSE History. I should also like to express my thanks to Roger Scruton for his helpful advice and constructive criticism, and to Barbara Day who gave invaluable practical assistance in producing the book.
The cover illustration is reproduced with the permission of the Mansell Collection.

INTRODUCTION

Joanna North

The new GCSE examination system which has recently been implemented in Britain's schools is the result of plans for reform which started in the 1970s. The calls for reform have come from within the teaching profession and from the countless advisers and other 'experts' within the educational system. Initially at least, the desire for change arose as a result of genuine concern about the way in which the two-tier system of GCE and CSE examinations was operating. Many teachers felt, for example, that the system was becoming too complex and, as a result, was failing to meet the needs of many children. Teachers had to select in advance those pupils who were felt capable of sitting the GCE examination; the grading system for a dual system had become extremely complex; and the problems were exacerbated by a shortage of resources which made it difficult for mixed-ability and single-ability teaching groups to be organised within a single school.

Despite the many policy documents, speeches and recommendations from the Schools Council, the National Union of Teachers (NUT) and other teaching unions, the call for a single system was not acted upon by the governments of the 1970s. It was not until 1982 that the then Secretary of State for Education, Sir Keith Joseph, announced the plans of the Conservative government for a single, national system of secondary education.

Many teachers and writers have expressed fears that the

educational system is now under central governmental
control to an extent that is unprecedented; while the fact
that the GCSE is a *Conservative* initiative has worried those
who fear a return to 'traditional' educational values, and an
undoing of the egalitarian ideology which has held sway for
the last two decades.

If one examines the philosophy which lies behind the
GCSE system, however, these fears may be seen to be
without foundation. The GCSE is in fact the natural result
of comprehensivisation and of the gradual destruction of
the grammar schools. In all important areas, the GCSE
incorporates and, in many cases, enlarges the scope of, the
egalitarian ideology which led to comprehensive secondary
education.

The 'New' Philosophy

The strongest attraction of the GCSE is its claim to be 'one
exam for all'. The new single system is to replace the dual
system of GCE and CSE. All courses are to conform to
national and subject-specific criteria decided upon by the
Department of Education and Science (DES). Proponents
of the GCSE claim that the national system will be fairer for
all children. No child should feel disadvantaged, since he
will be taking the same examination as his neighbour. There
will be no resentment towards those children who in the
past were bright enough to be entered for the GCE.

This basic egalitarian commitment is not overshadowed
by the fact that there will be differentiation *within* many of
the examinations themselves. In some subjects children will
be entered for papers which cater specifically for different
levels of ability, and in other subjects children will sit a
common paper which incorporates differentiated questions.
Many criticisms have been levelled at the system of

differentiation: some teachers feel that it merely duplicates the two-tier GCE/CSE hierarchy, but disguises the fact behind the façade of a single system. Less frequently heard is the criticism that the GCSE caters primarily for the low-ability child – out of the seven grades which may be achieved within the GCSE (A, B, C, D, E, F, G) it is grade F (almost the lowest) that is designed to reflect the abilities of the *average* child.

A more important criticism, however, and one that is expressed by many of the contributors to this book, is that the values and aims enshrined in the new examination will erode still further one of the most important goals of education – the pursuit of excellence. Those teachers who have taught in grammar schools and those parents and others who in the past have valued the GCE system for its emphasis on high standards and more formal teaching methods are beginning to recognise that the GCSE, far from raising standards overall, in fact guarantees that the education our children receive will move one step further down the road towards a state of general mediocrity.

The GCSE's commitment to an egalitarian programme is not the only value which has been transferred from the philosophy of comprehensivisation. The emphasis on child-centred learning, the use of mixed-ability teaching and informal teaching methods, the use of continuous assessment and coursework, and the aim of examining the child for what he 'knows, understands and can do' (in effect the abandonment of the concepts of pass and fail) – in all these ways the GCSE incorporates and reflects the idea that there should be less emphasis on merit, and more on equality.

In the final analysis the leftist, progressive educational orthodoxy of the 1960s and 1970s has been too powerful even for a Conservative administration. Against this orthodoxy not even the DES or the Government-appointed members of the Secondary Examinations Council (SEC) can prevail. The GCSE is a triumph for those who favour the destruction of the grammar school tradition and who desire to see the universities lose their long-established influence over the content and examination of secondary education.

One of the aims of this book, apart from the general aim of offering a contribution to the debate concerning the nature and value of secondary education, is to speak out, before it is too late, about the many worrying aspects of the new GCSE system and the philosophy which it enshrines. It is the hope of its contributors that something may still be done, either by individual parents and teachers, or by government, to maintain the respect for high standards and formal teaching methods which was one of the most valuable aspects of the GCE examination.

The Destruction of Traditional Teaching Methods

As every teacher knows, the aims and values enshrined in any particular examination system will affect the way courses are taught in schools. The GCSE is no exception to this rule. In many areas the GCSE National Criteria have changed the nature of education as it has traditionally been understood.

For example, the GCSE examination requires every subject to be assessed at least in part by coursework. Coursework may involve periodically or continuously assessed practical activities and project work. Teachers are to be responsible for carrying out assessments of their own pupils, and the National Criteria state that 'the teacher's judgement on the relationship between his or her own candidates should normally be accepted as correct'.

In itself the use of coursework in assessments is not a

completely new departure. Both CSE and GCE examinations have used coursework as a component in the past. But the *compulsory* core of coursework in the GCSE is a new feature. The emphasis on coursework embodies the recognition that some children find formal examinations more difficult than others. According to the egalitarian outlook, those children who suffer in this way are in an unfair position. Consequently examinations should cater for the needs of children who are held to perform better in 'less formal' conditions. The alternative point of view, that it is unfair to subject all children to the more frequent stress of periodic or continuous assessment, is one that is no longer mentioned.

The other attraction of coursework is that it offers to teachers greater opportunity for playing an important role in the design of syllabuses. Innovation and experimentation in the classroom have now become the order of the day. New subjects, or new emphases in already existing subjects, are now to be encouraged. In theory this might sound an exciting and welcome change. But in practice it is open to many objections.

One such objection is that the move away from traditional forms of assessment will inevitably mean that certain skills and abilities will no longer be valued so highly. As Jonathan Worthen points out in his essay on English teaching, the ability of a child to express himself clearly and precisely through discursive essays and summaries is to be replaced by such dubious skills as 'responding imaginatively' to a text. He argues that the GCSE represents an assault upon disciplined study, and indeed upon the whole process of the acquisition of genuine knowledge. He suggests that initiatives such as the compulsory use of coursework, show a wilful evasion on the part of educationists of the duty to give children a thorough education which can be tested by genuinely objective examination procedures.

The Threat to Specific Subjects

Some of the initiatives that are now enshrined in the GCSE system pose a threat not only to traditional methods of teaching, but to traditional school subjects themselves. This is not simply because new subjects like 'Integrated Humanities' and 'World Studies' have, in some schools, replaced subjects like English, History and Geography; it is also because the GCSE's emphasis on the acquisition of 'skills' and on the 'relevance' of syllabuses to the child's own experience, will involve some subjects becoming completely transformed.

In his article on GCSE History, Stewart Deuchar argues that History teaching in schools is undergoing just such a transformation. The philosophy lying behind the GCSE emphasises skills and relevance to the detriment of the *content* of History courses. As a result pupils no longer receive, through studying History, any sense of their own national heritage and culture.

A similar process may be observed in the teaching of Mathematics. Colin Coldman and Ken Shepherd chart the introduction of empirical methods into the traditional approach to Mathematics. The result is that this subject has become impoverished and empty. The GCSE, with its emphasis on practical mathematical experimentation and the acquisition of isolated skills, will tend towards the destruction of true mathematical understanding, leaving the child with a facile appreciation of numerical skills and a sketchy knowledge of the uses to which those 'skills' may be put in the real world.

Declining Standards

One of the aims of the GCSE is to improve standards generally and to help all pupils do better. Those who have designed the new system hope that standards will be raised if children are allowed to demonstrate a wider range of skills and practical abilities than those which have been examined in the past.

It might be argued that the emphasis on the acquisition of skills is of particular value in subjects like French, German and other modern languages. In addressing herself to the nature of modern language teaching under the GCSE system, however, Gisela M'Caw argues that, despite some positive and helpful innovations, the new modern language syllabuses have ignored or abandoned features which are of crucial importance if a child is to become reasonably competent in a foreign language. The use of translation and comprehension exercises, so important in learning a language, is no longer a compulsory element. Instead children are required to build up a simple list of disconnected words and phrases, and are not required (at the grade C level) to be able to combine these words and phrases into complete and meaningful sentences. As Gisela M'Caw argues, this failure to require a thorough training in language skills at the lower levels will mean that children who wish to aim at the higher grades will be at an extreme disadvantage. Once again we can see how the egalitarian philosophy underlying the GCSE will inevitably reward mediocrity at the expense of brighter children.

Simon Wyatt continues the criticism of 'skills acquisition' in his essay on GCSE Music. He argues that, although good teachers will still be free to maintain proper standards of Music teaching, the GCSE tends to emphasise activity and musical experience to the great detriment of musical knowledge. Mr Wyatt shows that here, as elsewhere, a simplistic and superficial approach to the subject is given preference over a rigorous and disciplined study of works of the highest quality. The result is no less than an assault on our musical tradition – one of the most precious heritages of Western civilisation – from within the ranks of those appointed to preserve it.

The Death of Liberal Education?

The essays in the first part of the book deal with the ways in which specific subjects are under threat from the new examination system. In Part 2, Anthony O'Hear and Hywel Williams address themselves to the more general question, of how far the idea of a liberal and humane education is threatened by the new initiative.

According to Professor O'Hear, the GCSE represents an abandonment of the traditional idea of education as an 'initiation into existing forms of worthwhile knowledge and understanding'. The acquisition of 'skills' and the exploration of 'relevant' topics are regarded as more important than the learning of facts, and more important than a firm appreciation of the nation's cultural heritage. What we are about to lose as a result of the GCSE system is the vision which perceives knowledge and the disinterested pursuit of truth as inherently valuable in the development of a humane and sensitive outlook upon the world. Unless something can be done to preserve this vision, perhaps through the introduction of another, more academic, examination, one can only fear that the decline in the quality of education which we have witnessed over the last few years will continue unabated.

Hywel Williams echoes the fears expressed by O'Hear

when he argues that the GCSE's emphasis on neutral 'skills' of interpretation and evaluation, far from ensuring that education will be free from elitist conceptions of knowledge, in fact replaces one set of preferences with those of the professional 'educators' of the day. Any education of skills in fact presupposes a set of values and choices which are historically and culturally rooted. The fault of the new skill-based education is that it tries to divorce the acquisition of these skills from the culture and history which alone make them meaningful and valuable. In a more secure age skills *were* taught, but not explicitly and consciously – they were taught through the very process of initiating the child into a cultural heritage. As Hywel Williams notes, the modern emphasis on 'skills education' indicates the extent to which that secure world, together with its culture and self-confidence, has been destroyed. If we are to teach children skills it can take place only in the context of a wide and coherent body of recognised knowledge, such as is provided by the tradition of humane education. The pursuit of knowledge within an environment of stable, disciplined order, should be our aim. Williams touches here upon the central value of the public school tradition, which offered the possibility of creative and imaginative insight precisely because the educational atmosphere was one which embraced institutional order and stability.

The Politicisation of Education

Perhaps the most worrying aspect of the GCSE is the extent to which it allows, indeed encourages, the politicisation of education. Over the last few years we have witnessed the spectacle of education becoming a pawn within a battleground of political intrigue. The seeds of war were sown in the 1960s and in the early 1970s when leftist and progressivist forces turned their attention to the sphere of education. The results of progressive educational ideology are manifest in the GCSE's fear of 'bias' of all kinds, in its scorn of excellence and achievement, and in its stipulation that children are to acquire a 'positive attitude' towards other cultures and ethnic groups (although no comparable attitude to their own national culture and history).

David Cooper examines the new politicised curriculum in his essay on Multicultural Education. The commitment to the recognition and appreciation of cultural diversity is written into the GCSE in its National Criteria, to which all syllabuses are to conform. Cooper argues that this emphasis will affect and in some cases completely transform, the teaching of many subjects. The aim is to incorporate a 'pluralist perspective' into every school subject, with the purported aims of combatting 'racism' and of enriching a child's education with an understanding of ethnic minority cultures. Professor Cooper questions the assumptions, aims and methods of Multicultural Education – the claim that Britain *is* a multicultural society, the assumption that children may be 'enriched' through the kind of teaching which is offered by the radical reformer, and the belief that such teaching is of great educational value.

In fact, as Professor Cooper argues, the kind of curriculum which is proposed by those in favour of Multicultural Education is one which is profoundly *counter*-educational: no adequate understanding of another culture can be achieved before a child has a sufficient grasp of his *own* tradition. But, as has been argued by other contributors to this book, the sensitive appreciation of British culture and British ways of life is precisely what is likely to disappear from education if the philosophy of the GCSE is successfully implemented. At best the insistence on a multicultural perspective will destroy that sensitivity of outlook and tolerance of other peoples which traditional education, when most successful, encouraged and nurtured. At worst the new politicised curriculum will be profoundly antagonising, serving to accentuate and magnify that which divides us. The explicit commitment to Multicultural Education gives to proponents of 'anti-racism' the permission to pursue their fanatical, and in truth, hate-filled, policies of censorship and thought-control.

In the penultimate chapter I chart the politicisation of the curriculum in more detail, drawing attention to the commitment within the national and subject-specific criteria, not only to multiculturalism, but also to anti-sexism, and to the avoidance of political and 'other forms of bias'. As I try to show, the commitment to the avoidance of bias, together with an emphasis on relevance and the awareness of economic, social, political and environmental issues, opens the doors to a fully politicised curriculum, within which the radical left is free to argue for its own causes. My suggestion is that the teaching of controversial issues in schools should, if at all possible, be avoided. In those situations where a teacher cannot avoid touching upon some sensitive issue, such as homosexuality, arms control or food distribution, steps should be taken to ensure that the materials used are properly balanced and representative. There should be standards of good teaching practice drawn up which require a teacher to refrain from expressing his own political views.

Positive Proposals

Most of the contributors to this collection of essays have accepted that the GCSE is here to stay. While drawing attention to those aspects of the new examination system which they feel are inadequate and destructive of a sound education they have, for the most part, been content to rely upon the integrity and sensitivity of individual classroom teachers to ensure that a subject is taught adequately, and that the children within their care learn as much as they can and achieve the highest standards possible to them in the allotted time. No doubt there are many dedicated teachers who will endeavour to carry out their tasks to the best of their abilities: to continue, as they have always done, to bring out the best in their pupils.

The overall thrust of the argument in these pages, however, is that the GCSE poses a severe threat to real education. In the name of an egalitarian programme, emphasising practical skills and a training for life in the adult world, the GCSE is in fact deeply anti-educational. Much that was of value in the old system will be lost forever – the commitment to excellence; the recognition of the value of properly acquired factual knowledge; the view of knowledge as a cumulative process, built one step upon another, with a thorough grounding in basic skills of reading, writing and comprehension; the respect for knowledge whose 'relevance' cannot be easily perceived; and an appreciation of the time-honoured values and principles of tolerance and self-respect enshrined within our national culture. The loss of these elements from the educational process must be of deep concern to all those who care about education.

If, as is likely, the quality of education will be further eroded by the GCSE it may be wondered whether the individual teacher alone can do much to halt the general decline. It is surely appropriate at this time, before the damage is irreversible, to suggest the introduction of alternative measures, supported by government and recognised by the teaching profession.

One such alternative is suggested by Nicholas Debenham in the final essay in this book. On behalf of those who wish their children to receive a thorough education based on tried and trusted methods and the study of central academic subjects, he recommends the introduction of an alternative examination and a 'core curriculum'. This curriculum would be taught between the ages 10 and 16, and no specialisation would be allowed until after that age. Each child would study, along traditional lines, the same set of subjects. Nicholas Debenham sets out the basic content of each subject in a clear and precise manner. Although he does not suggest exactly how such an alternative examination could be implemented, it is clear, as he says, that it is likely to appeal to independent schools and those which are already alive to the value of traditional English education. It may be that those schools who now have the chance of 'opting out' of local authority control and receiving grants directly from the government could also be offered the opportunity of adopting the 'alternative' examination.

However it might be implemented, the idea of an alternative examination, associated with a core curriculum, offers real hope for the future of British schools. No doubt it will be resisted by many, and criticised as a return to 'elitist' values. But such resistance should itself be critically examined. Would it come from parents or, as is more likely, from the self-styled 'experts' – from advisers and leftist educational writers? If the latter then can we be sure that the child's best interests are being served, or is it not the case that our children are being once again manipulated by those who have a vested interest in maintaining control over the ideology and the aims of national education?

PART ONE

PART ONE

1. ENGLISH

Jonathan Worthen

With the end of the academic year, 1986-1987, the O-Level ends its existence, those having taken the examination in the summer of 1987 being the last to do so. For the foreseeable future, the GCSE, the courses for which began in September 1986, will be the new secondary examination system at school-leaving age, replacing both the O-Level and the CSE, and covering the entire ability range formerly covered by these two systems.

The fact that the new examining system is now upon us is due to the activity of the Department of Education and Science under the direction of its former minister, Sir Keith Joseph. This is not to say that Sir Keith created the examination (it is actually the creation of educationists and, supposedly, teachers, and has been fermenting for a good many years); but it is his will and energy that have brought in the examination as a mandatory innovation. The introduction of the new system has been undoubtedly accelerated by the emergence of education as an important political (and, of course, electoral) issue. The present Conservative administration is anxious to show concern over the state system (whose defects have become glaringly apparent as comprehensivisation has become the order of the day), and the introduction of the GCSE is a major attempt to be seen to be doing something to improve the general situation.

It is, however, my contention that the new examination

system will further erode the standards that comprehensivisation has already eroded; I believe, in fact, that a real analogy exists between the destruction of the grammar schools by a past Labour administration and the abolition of the O-Level by the present Conservative government. Indeed, the Conservative vandalism is even worse than that perpetrated by Labour, for grammar schools and independent schools still exist within a majority comprehensive system, but the new GCSE will be compulsory everywhere, in comprehensive, grammar and independent alike. The abolition of the O-Level, which was in essence the grammar school examination and hence the controller of the grammar school curriculum, means the destruction of the grammar school system of study, even if the schools as institutions continue to exist. The fact that a Conservative administration is engineering this radical change is an irony that will doubtless prove bitter to the true Conservative just as it will be amusing the Socialist.

What I have to say about the nature of the GCSE examination and why I believe it to be a deleterious development will be confined to my own specialism as a subject teacher, English. However, I have no doubt that the tendency which underlies the new examination in English can be discerned in other areas also. The first point about the new examination (and its chief selling point) is that it is one examination for all. Why this is a selling point can be simply explained in terms of popular egalitarianism, which has much in common with old-fashioned envy, and it is the same basic selling point which was used for the comprehensive system. (Indeed, the new examination *is* the comprehensive school examination *par excellence*.) No parent will now be disconcerted by the fact that his or her child is doing an examination which explicitly caters for a lower ability range than another parent's child. Everyone will be entered for GCSE, not O-Level (the brighter ones) and CSE (the less able ones) as before, so at least until the results come out the difference in ability is not revealed.

Now, even though the new examination has one title only, in a number of subjects different papers catering for different levels of ability will continue to be set; pupils of different ability levels being entered for the different papers. In English, however, there will be no such distinction; instead, both in 'English Literature' and 'English' a common paper will be given to all ability levels. The term 'differentiation by outcome'[1] is used to explain how pupils of widely varying intelligence will continue to demonstrate their different capacities: if all pupils are given a common question, the kinds of answers produced (ranging from very profound and detailed to shallow and sketchy) will reveal different ability levels. This is of course true for certain kinds of questions and is no new discovery of modern educational theory, but there are disturbing implications underlying this common-paper, common-question method that need to be examined. For if all pupils are to be able even to understand the questions on the examination paper, then the language must be very simple indeed. Those involved in the devising of the GCSE have obviously been aware of this issue, as evidenced by the following extract on the subject of Literature examination questions from the Secondary Examinations Council official booklet on GCSE English:

> ... traditional discursive essay questions using key words and phrases such as 'discuss', 'describe', 'character sketch', 'give an account of' may be less readily interpreted by students lower down the ability range, and may therefore fail to provide equivalent opportunities for all candidates to show the knowledge and understanding they possess.[2]

Now, language is not some mere cloak thrown over thoughts but the vehicle of thought itself. If 'traditional discursive essay' language is discarded in questions, then the traditional discursive essay itself will tend to disappear. The fact that certain bright pupils at certain schools may well continue to use the language of literary criticism and to apply it even when a question is couched in another kind of language does not invalidate the danger, because the growing tendency will be in many schools to jettison forms of language and, therefore, thought, that do not appear on an examination paper. For the type of examination that is set always dictates the nature of the course to be followed, and the type of examination we have here is clearly a levelled-down examination, which will tend to result in a levelling-down of teaching and performance.

So far as the language of passages upon which questions are set is concerned, the situation is somewhat more complex. A levelling-down tendency will clearly operate, as is evidenced by a passage from the colloquially written Adrian Mole books on the London and East Anglian Group specimen English paper. However, examiners will find it impossible to avoid passages that contain a certain degree of sophistication and difficulty, because there has to be at least something for the brighter candidates to delve into in order to produce the more profound answers that will justify the 'differentiation of outcome' at which the common-question method is supposed to aim. The result, I believe, is that the language of passages set for commentary, summary and comprehension will tend to cater for what might broadly be termed the middle area of ability, neither stretching the best adequately nor being within the reach of the worst. Such is the consequence of a common examination-paper system: a tendency to focus upon the capacities of the mediocre, with the inevitable levelling-down which that tendency involves.

This matter of levelling-down is at the very heart of the new examination's attitude to English Literature. As it happens, 'English Literature' will continue to be a separate course from 'English'; but this very separation is challenged by egalitarian educationists, and by teachers who wish to see the end of English Literature as a separate area of study. For English Literature, as traditionally understood, is a subject which can be studied properly only by a few – by the top two or three sets or streams in a year, say, assuming the school has setting or streaming. This is not to say that English Literature has no part in a curriculum for the less able (indeed, I believe that great literature is an essential element in a curriculum for all abilities), but that the kind of mind needed to indulge in and benefit from the critical study of English Literature as traditionally conceived is simply not found across the whole ability range. The egalitarian understands this and dislikes it, and is therefore eager to abolish English Literature as a study in its own right. By abolishing it and incorporating its attenuated residue into a general English course the egalitarian would achieve his aim of destroying an 'élitist' subject. He has not won – yet – but he is still hoping to do so; and the abolition of the O-Level system may well provide him with the opportunity. (The continuing existence of A-Level English is a bulwark against such change, but I fear that it is a bulwark that will henceforth come under increasing attack.) Even if English Literature in the GCSE remains at the moment a separate area, the ground for its removal is already prepared with the compulsory inclusion of a diluted literary study element in the 'English' course (note how the term 'English Language' has vanished) and with the removal of 'traditional discursive essay' language in the question-setting already discussed. As I have already argued, the removal of this kind of language has a natural tendency to destroy the 'traditional discursive essay' itself, an essay style at one point characterised pejoratively in the Secondary Examinations Council booklet as 'the conventional "Law Court" approach to literature'.[3]

The aim of the GCSE is in fact to breed out traditional literary study by surrounding it with a mish-mash of other 'ways of responding' to literature:

> The 'scholarly' essay characteristic of many GCE O-Level examination questions is only one way of responding to literary texts and of demonstrating appreciation and understanding of their structure, meaning and style. Responding to literature (and to non-literary texts for that matter) can be thought of as a process which involves the reader in a 'dialogue' with the text.[4]

Thus, as the Secondary Examinations Council booklet goes on to illustrate, the new GCSE pupil may engage in meaningful 'dialogue' with, say, *The Crucible*, by writing a radio script based on 'the anti-Communist witch-hunt of the 1950s':

> *Interviewer*: Our first guest is Mickey Spillane, author of 'I, the Jury', 'One Lonely Night', and 'The Big Kill', amongst others; stories about the tough private eye, Mike Hammer, who killed for justice and democracy. A typical scene from one of his books reads:
> *Narrator*: 'I killed more people tonight than I have fingers on my hands. I shot them in cold blood and enjoyed every minute of it ... they were commies, Lee. They were Red sons-of-bitches who should have died long ago .... They never thought that there were people like me in this country. They figure us all to be soft as horse manure and just as stupid.'[5]

The tendentious purpose of such material as the above is so obvious that it does not need to be spelled out.

Of course, this emphasis on other 'ways of responding to literary texts' is not new. (In fact, little about GCSE is new; its 'ideas' have been in circulation since the sixties. What is new is that these ideas are now *de rigueur* for all.) Frank Whitehead, who in the mid-sixties pleased progressive English teachers with his book *The Disappearing Dais*, had by the mid-seventies realised that this style of teaching led to the destruction of a proper appreciation of literature:

> Increasingly literature has been 'used' – 'used' to propagate a social or political message ... 'used' to illustrate a pre-determined theme such as 'Witchcraft' (bring in an extract from *Macbeth*) or 'Colour Prejudice' (duplicate copies of *A Little Black Boy*); 'used' ... as a launching-pad to get children talking or writing about their own experiences .... All these now fashionable activities seem to me to imply an erosion of belief in the power of literature as such, in the value of exposing oneself to the impact of a poem or story or novel for its own sake. At its worst the approach seems to carry with it an assumption that anything a pupil says or writes after reading a work of literature must somehow be relevant to it....[6]

This was written in 1976, yet now, more than ten years on, the progressive ideas attacked by Whitehead are enshrined in a new compulsory examination, promoted by a Conservative government!

And what of the actual literary texts themselves? How do they fare in the GCSE? We learn from the Secondary Examinations Council booklet that the GCSE General Criteria require that all examinations be 'free of political, ethnic, gender and other forms of bias' and that they should recognise 'the linguistic and cultural diversity of society'.[7] The booklet states that 'one of the particular implications for English Literature is that the traditional "canon" of English Literature will be widened' and that the teacher

must 'make sure ... that the range of texts offered relates
equally to the interests and experiences of girls and boys,
and meets the requirements for ethnic and political
balance'.[8]

Of course, any sensitive and civilised teacher will choose
the texts he is teaching with tact and discretion, bearing in
mind the nature of his pupils, but the GCSE Criteria cited
above have nothing to do with such matters of traditional
common sense and decency. They are, quite obviously, an
aspect of that current tyranny which has already driven
honourable teachers from their posts and which thought-
polices whole professions, namely the threat of being
labelled a 'sexist' or a 'racist'. And as for 'political balance',
what exactly might this mean in practice? In the present
climate it would not be taking too wild a flight of fancy to
suppose that it would justify the inclusion of overtly radical
writers to counter-balance 'right wing' figures like Jane
Austen and Shakespeare.

Furthermore, 'set texts need no longer be prescribed'[9] in
the GCSE. In the London and East Anglian Group
syllabus, for example, there are no set texts for detailed
study; instead, very general questions are given which
pupils may answer in relation to any texts from a broad list,
and all texts are permitted in the examination room. Some
boards admittedly still have Literature papers which do
examine set texts, but there is always the option of doing
100% coursework instead of taking an examination, and a
number of syllabuses allow texts to be taken into the
examination room, following the precedent of the 'plain
texts' O-Level Literature, highly regarded by GCSE pun-
dits as a progressive examination. In all of this we see a
movement away from the traditional requirement of English Literature, that specific texts must be studied in detail
and known so well that significant sections are committed to

memory. Such traditional requirements have been under attack by the progressive consensus of the last twenty odd years: in this respect as in others the GCSE can be seen as providing recognition of progresive ideas as the new official orthodoxy. In its assault upon knowledge and memory, it seems to me, the decline of English Literature as a subject can be clearly foreseen. Professor John Carey, in an article written some ten years ago, made the following pertinent remarks:

> The most doctrinaire opponent of rote-learning still requires practitioners (of surgery) to be knowledgeable, and thoroughly tested, before they are let loose on his intestines. But in literature, history, and allied disciplines, the traditional timed examination, which genuinely tested knowledge, has been largely abandoned, and replaced by course-assessment, open-book tests, and other evasions, where the student's task is to cover large quantities of paper with words that have never, so far as one can tell, passed anywhere near his retentive faculties.[10]

The progressives, who now have in the GCSE the encapsulation of their doctrines, would claim to lay stress on understanding rather than knowledge. But the fact is that knowledge is the necessary prerequisite to understanding. To quote Professor Carey again:

> Schools and universities are supposed to promote informed discussion ... (and) students who are to engage in informed discussion must have memories that are trained and equipped. Indeed, to place young people in situations where discussion is expected is thoroughly unfair, unless this training and equipping has been undertaken. Finding themselves reduced to grunts and opinionativeness, they will inevitably feel frustrated, and so opt for less demanding pursuits like smashing up university buildings or assaulting visiting speakers.[11]

An examination course, such as the GCSE in English
Literature, that does not insist unequivocally that memory
is an essential and highly valued art, and therefore worth
testing in some detail, seems to me to indicate a lost sense of
the true value of the subject under study. For to learn by
heart is to take to heart, to possess as part of oneself some
area of valued knowledge: not to see the importance of this
learning is not truly to value the knowledge itself.

This failure to appreciate that a sure foundation of
knowledge is necessary before true understanding can begin
indicates a faulty pedagogy, or even a total absence of
pedagogy. Those who are behind the GCSE English
Literature claim that their emphasis upon coursework
rather than set texts makes for a broad understanding, with
pupils able to explore a variety of literature, making
connections, tracing themes, freed from the 'narrow specialisation' of the traditional O-Level style. Now, what we
have here is an ignorance of pedagogic method, a failure to
grasp that learning to walk precedes learning to run, and
certainly precedes complex balletic steps. The mind that is
able to explore widely in literature with any degree of
sureness and success emerges over a period of time, perhaps
not truly existing until post-graduate level. And such a mind
is created by a pedagogy that begins with teaching pupils
fundamentals properly before it introduces them to speculation and research. The traditional approach to English
Literature provided such a pedagogy: teaching pupils
certain specific texts surely and thoroughly, while at the
same time introducing them to other, non-set texts, this
latter process gradually expanding through the O-Level
course into A-Level, where it really begins to flourish. The
new approach, that of the GCSE, is of course the 'project'
type, seemingly attractive in its claims to 'breadth' and its
folders bulging with 'pupil-researched' extended essays, but

in fact showing superficial understanding, lack of focus and direction, and with the material imperfectly assimilated or not assimilated at all, because it is folder material, not material for the mind.

The character Clym Yeobright, in Hardy's *Return of the Native* bears a close similarity to the minds behind GCSE English Literature. He talks of his education plan (happily never realised) for the rustics of Egdon Heath, in terms that show a lofty dismissal of the actual processes of mental development:

> My plan is one for instilling high knowledge into empty minds without first cramming them with what has to be uncrammed again before true study begins.[12]

Clym is a character from fiction: unfortunately, the devisers of the GCSE are not only creatures of the real world but are the hierophants of the new orthodoxy.

So far, we have used the term 'examination' when referring to the GCSE, but as we have seen already, this is in fact a misnomer, for one of the radical elements of GCSE is the compulsory use of coursework as a means of assessment. Again, the use of coursework in assessment is not new: the practice has been in existence for a number of years. What is new is its compulsory introduction into every subject. In English, in fact, it is possible to do 'English' and 'English Literature' *entirely* by coursework! Quite how a final result based on 100% coursework can be compared with a result based on 50% coursework, 50% examination, is a question of great importance, involving as it does the business of true assessment, justice, and standards. But, as I shall show, it is a question that is irrelevant to the kind of egalitarian thinking behind GCSE English. Without conducting a full debate on the question of coursework versus examination, the consideration of a few basic points should bring us to the heart of the matter.

Firstly, no man should be a judge in his own cause. But this is inevitably what the teacher becomes if he is involved in the assessment of his own pupils' work. This is not to say that teachers, either *en masse* or in isolated cases, will falsify results so as to promote their own pupils' interests. Rather, it is to say that they should not be asked to perform a role which is, properly speaking, beyond their professional capacity. Unlike the teacher involved in directing his pupils' work, a trained assessor has the time, expertise, and objective distance to compare different results.

Secondly, the conditions under which the coursework is produced surely have to be stringently controlled if the work is seen to be evidence of the individual pupil's ability alone. But this is simply not the case in GCSE English, as only one or at most 'some' pieces (depending on syllabus) are to be done under 'controlled conditions' (which 'need not however be equated with "examination conditions"'!).[13] The rest is done at home or at school, supervised or not, with no specified time-limit. (Admittedly, a form must be signed by pupil and teacher to say that the work is the pupil's own; but the honesty of such a deposition by a pupil cannot be verified.) Perhaps more important is the fact that, while there are broad stipulations in GCSE English as to the nature of coursework, there are no common questions that must be answered at all. Quite the opposite in fact; for the teacher is encouraged to teach freely, and to let the work for assessment grow out of the lessons. Exactly how can pieces of work of such enormous variety (and done under such different conditions) possibly be compared for purposes of assessment? They cannot, of course. And here, I believe, we come to the egalitarian principle at the heart of the GCSE. True assessment (objective, fair, with pupil measured against pupil) cannot take place in such a system, and because this is so, assessment is devalued and becomes a sham. Your 'A' is of no more significance than my 'D'. (This devaluation is quite definitely desired by a number of teachers and educationists, who can be heard saying such things as that examination results are 'pieces of paper desired by middle-class parents'!) It is no wonder that some proponents of the GCSE stress that what they call 'process' (work assignments set over two years) is as important as, or even more important than, 'product' (final competence which can actually be assessed).

In containing elements of compulsory coursework the GCSE is just like the old CSE, and it also follows CSE in its compulsory oral element. Indeed, the comparison with CSE (the lower ability examination which was originally devised for those who could not cope with O-Level) is a very pertinent one, for it shows just what kind of examination (essentially non-academic) the GCSE is. Many teachers in my acquaintance, after a reading of any of the GCSE English material, have said, in effect, 'But this is CSE writ large!' The oral element to this new examination borrowed from CSE practice is, I maintain, a particularly meretricious feature of the new system. Its supposed attractiveness is obvious; and yet it is opposed, I maintain, to real learning. Many people are taken by the 'practical' merits of oral English. (Sir Keith Joseph was apparently very keen.) After all, aren't we speaking all day long, and for so many purposes, often so obviously useful? And isn't it the case that many pupils will pass from school into lives of work and leisure that will involve very little written English, but much spoken English? Well, yes to both questions; but it does not follow that oral English is a subject for major study in school English lessons. To begin with, the undeniable fact that we speak so much means that we are practised in many of the uses of oral English already, and in real contexts that simply cannot be manufactured in school. Frank Palmer, in his excellent essay 'English: Reducing Learning to Short-Cut "Skills"' says something relevant here, when he remarks about the inappropriateness of trying to train pupils in 'telephone skills' at school:

> All the role-play in the world will not give pupils what is required to say something of any consequence on a telephone: common-sense, a good all-round academic education, naturally-matured relationships and the knowledge and experience of working (in a bank, in a travel agent's office) which comes not from simulation but from experience.[14]

But the GCSE devisers have a concept of oral English that goes beyond learning how to speak well in different situations: they conceive of it as a farrago of all different kinds of speech, no matter how limited and colloquial, addressed to all different kinds of audiences. Even desultory chit-chat to a friend has its place in such a relativistic mélange. I would argue that good spoken English results from good teaching based on written English. The higher forms of the written language would be then imprinted to some degree on the spoken, obviously not making the two forms of language identical, but levelling up the vaguer, more inaccurate form of spoken language to the standards of the more precise and accurate written form. It is the exact opposite of this – a levelling-down of written English to the standard of a sloppy colloquial – that is the modern trend, now enshrined in the GCSE. Not inappropriate here are the words of a recent A-Level report on candidates' written language, a written language reduced to the level of casual spoken English:

It is felt that candidates sometimes have insufficient practice
in writing and that in the examination room almost for the
first time, some of them find themselves having to turn their
ideas not into debating points in discussion, but into
sentences and paragraphs.... In a cliché-ridden world, it is
not expected that candidates can keep their language robust
and pristine, but there is a lower depth into which it is fatal
to stumble, a depth where expression is so slovenly and
sloppy that it becomes meaningless.... (A-Level) argument
needs to be conducted in a language suitable for communication between candidate and examiner – what used,
once upon a time, to be called educated English. If the
present downward trend continues amongst some of the
weaker candidates, there are going to be two languages (to
add to two cultures, two nations etc.): English as it is written
in works of literature, and English as it is spoken colloquially now – a kind of basic communication, language used like
a nudge or a nod, part noise, part signal.[15]

It seems to me to be a natural feature of what I consider to
be a levelling-down, essentially unacademic examination
system, that spoken English – often loose, disconnected,
thoughtless, emotional and error-ridden – should assume an
important part, dominating lesson-time, turning the classroom into a Babel, making for disruption, and crowding
out the teacher's voice.

We move here to the whole organisation of the modern
comprehensive classroom. Traditionally, individual pupils
faced a teacher and listened. Now groups of pupils face each
other around tables and talk. The devaluing of the teacher
as an authority (both on his subject and as a controller of
classroom discipline) is implicit in the new classroom
arrangement and in the whole GCSE style. Implicit also is
the idea that the GCSE is the examination which will make
mixed-ability teaching a widespread practice. For a single
examination (in English at any rate) will give the excuse,
which will be readily seized upon, not to set or stream

pupils: the use in the Secondary Examinations Council booklet of such modish language as providing 'classroom activities' and 'inviting' pupils 'to undertake different tasks suited to their own level of ability'[16] points clearly to a heterogeneous class that is not taught as a class. Indeed, the word 'teach' is quite inappropriate here, for in mixed-ability 'teaching' (which is insinuated to be the GCSE style) the teacher is a manager of 'tasks' and 'activities', not a teacher as traditionally conceived – an acknowledged authority uniquely qualified to disseminate knowledge and cultivate understanding, an inspiring presence who, in Frank Palmer's words, 'will want to acquaint his pupils with the best and most beautiful things he knows'.[17] Such a teacher will, I fear, be 'extinguished for ever' (to use Edmund Burke's famous phrase) in the classroom of the future. There are few indeed left already.

At the beginning of this paper it was said that a prime motive in the present Government's bringing in of the GCSE was its concern to be seen to be doing something to improve the state of things in education, and Sir Keith Joseph and other voices have suggested that the new examination will serve to improve standards. Now, improving standards is obviously desirable, and a little careful thinking will reveal that there are three broad ways in which actual examination results (as an objective measurement of standards) can be improved. The first is by having a better quality of teaching for the existing examination syllabuses; the second is by somehow having a better quality of pupils; and the third is by changing the nature of the examination itself so as to make it easier. (It is dishonest to confuse the last point with the first, as some have done by saying that changing the nature of the examination will make for better teaching. As a hypothesis, this could be so; but it is simply not verifiable, because there is no 'constant' factor in the experiment.)

If, as Sir Keith Joseph and others fondly seem to believe, the GCSE will raise standards, then one is driven to suspect that this new examination will be easier than the previous systems. This is in fact no idle speculation, as a reading of the GCSE's words on 'differentiation' will serve to show. This new bold examination, apparently, will no longer 'discriminate' as the old order used to do, but will, we are told, 'differentiate'. And what exactly does this special new process entail? The answer, for what it is worth, is that the new system will be a 'radical departure from some current practice where it could be argued that many candidates achieve their marks by relative failure at tasks and where, as a result, they may complete only a small part of the paper successfully'. Henceforth, examinations will be a 'positive' experience where candidates are 'encouraged to demonstrate what they know, understand and can do'.[18] Winston Churchill's words are jubilantly quoted by the GCSE proponents (the mention of Churchill doubtless helps to disarm Conservative sceptics!):

> I should have liked to be asked to say what I knew. They always tried to ask what I did not know. When I would have willingly displayed my knowledge, they sought to expose my ignorance. This sort of treatment had only one result: I did not do well in examinations.

Churchill or not, I make bold to say that all this is sheer humbug. Any good examination gives candidates the chance to 'display (their) knowledge', but in response to the actual questions set on the paper. If a candidate is to gain marks for simply 'displaying' a portion of knowledge, irrespective of whether it is asked for or not, then an examination has not tested whether the whole syllabus has been taught, assimilated and understood, with candidates being measured against each other accurately and fairly, in other words the examination has been deprived of its raison d'être. A true examination, despite what the GCSE proponents say, *is* about 'relative failure' or, what is another way of saying the same thing, 'relative success'. *If* what the GCSE proponents mean is that an examination system that purports to test the whole ability range must set very different papers for candidates of different ability levels, the lower level papers gaining lower grades than the higher level, then this is at least sense. But this cannot be the meaning; for such was the system with O-Level and CSE, and the GCSE devisers are talking of a 'radical departure' from previous ways. No, I fear that any meaning that actually lies behind the GCSE's euphemistic words about examinations being a 'positive experience' is that the GCSE will be easier to pass. If this is so, and the GCSE produces a crop of higher grades than the previous system, then the whole massive exercise will supposedly be justi-fied: criticism, at least from large areas of the general public, will be disarmed.

But what of criticism from the teaching profession itself? Some opposition to the GCSE has been expressed, but this has been in the context of disputes over pay, and has taken the form of a clamour for more time and 'resources', were the new system to be put into practice. This clamour still exists, but it has nothing to do with the objections that I have raised. Indeed, as has been pointed out many times, 'teachers have been wanting a new system like this for years'.

A volume of essays such as this will doubtless provide evidence that not all those concerned with education are happy with the recent 'reforms'. Indeed, my belief is that there are many others who think and feel the same but who are driven to silence by a form of insidious collective coercion that forbids what is termed 'negative' comment. To put it in very blunt terms, a 'negative' reaction to the GCSE is hardly a recommendation for promotion. But not to articulate a keenly felt disquiet about a proposed radical change would be wrong indeed. For it would amount to an assumption that critical thought, if contrary to the prevailing *Zeitgeist*, is outlawed. In a free society, such an assumption would indeed be intolerable.

Clearly, my own reaction to the implications of the new examination in English is a highly critical one, though this is not to say that I have been happy with all that existed at O-Level and CSE. For example, the great variety of syllabuses and, more important, standards among the different O-Level and CSE boards has always seemed to me to be in need of some regulation. Nevertheless, the GCSE, despite the boast that it will achieve through its supposed 'single examination system' a desirable uniformity of standards, has simply created a new array of different syllabuses. As I have argued, assessment is now, far from being improved, actually confused and devalued. I would have wished to see emerging from a single examination system some test of basic competence in English Language for all pupils. This could be taken, say, at third year level by the most able, while other pupils would take it, and retake it if necessary, at later stages up to school-leaving age. The contents of such an examination have already been suggested by the HMSO booklet *English from 5 to 16: Curriculum Matters 1* (1984). It is true that this booklet, with its championing of the teaching of basic English and its stress upon clear assessment, has been received with hostility by many voices in the teaching profession. But I would hold out some small hope that, under Mr Baker, who has shown an interest in English teaching, an examination such as I have alluded to would not be an impossible reform. People exist outside the teaching profession who could turn their minds to such matters – Dr Robert Burchfield and Anthony Burgess, for example, both of whom have written recently on the subject of English teaching.[19] The place for a common examination is, however, only at a basic level. When (and only when) pupils had demonstrated their competence at it, they would move on to different courses and examinations, in English Language and/or English Literature, according to their ability. Such a scheme of education, needless to say, would be contrary to the egalitarian ethos of GCSE English.

In the meantime, what is one to do? For those teachers who are critical of the implications of GCSE English, I would counsel a firm adherence to the excellence that they believe in and have traditionally sought to foster. Within the broad ambit of the GCSE it is, I think, still possible to adhere to traditional pedagogy and standards, though these will be increasingly under attack, especially within the comprehensive-dominated state sector. To focus one's mind upon A-Level English is a useful guide, at least for one's best pupils: the English teacher must strive to cultivate as many pupils capable of taking A-Level as he did before under the O-Level. And for those pupils who do not possess such capacities, the teacher's job should continue to be what it always has been: to produce as high a standard of literacy within each pupil as he can manage to attain.

However, matters may not prove so simple. Voices are now being heard which argue that the abolition of A-Level must follow from the abolition of O-Level. If, as seems all too probable, this is being seriously contemplated by those in authority, then matters in education are bleak indeed. The levelling-down process will then take over the whole school system, from where it will inevitably leap into higher education. Those concerned to shore up what is left, now that O-Level has gone, must resist as strongly as they can any proposals for a 'GCSE Stage 2' to replace the A-Level.

And finally, what can parents do, who are concerned about the new system? First, they can make their voices heard on the matter just dealt with, the possible future abolition of A-Levels: the existence of these is at the moment the only bulwark against the drop in standards inherent in the single system of GCSE. Secondly, parents must speak out against the argument that many schools and subject departments will now deploy – namely, that GCSE obviates the need for any setting or streaming, and accordingly that mixed-ability teaching is the order of the day. Thirdly, parents should be wary of relativistic arguments about literary texts chosen by English departments, especially if their children are A-Level material: the best authors should be insisted upon, and a Shakespeare play should be a *sine qua non*. Fourthly, parents should not let themselves be blinded by the supposed science of any new examination or course of study when discussing their children's education with teachers: common-sense questions about fundamentals such as 'I'm worried about his/her spelling. What can be done about this?' should be asked fearlessly, and intelligible answers should be expected and insisted upon. Lastly, if a school or department does not seem to be teaching to a standard that parents are satisfied with, and it is impossible for the children to be taken elsewhere, then parents should not be afraid to seek to remedy the deficiencies at home. For when all is said and done, if an educational system is felt to be inadequate, and it is the only system on offer, then one's own resources are all that one has to fill the gap, and one has a duty to use these resources as well as one can.

2. HISTORY

Stewart Deuchar

'We cannot escape from history. Our lives are governed by what happened in the past, our decisions by what we believe to have happened.'[1] Thus Professor Marwick of the Open University, and he is surely right. But the present reality is that we are raising our children with little or no historical knowledge.

Not so long ago a school was a school and a teacher was a teacher and history was – more or less – history. Things were no doubt far from ideal, but there was general agreement that some knowledge of the history of one's country was an essential attribute of an 'educated person'.

Now all is changed. In the last two decades, the concept of an 'educated person', as the hoped-for end product of the education system, has disappeared without trace in the wholesale debasement of our culture. Moreover, during this period traditional teachers of history have found themselves increasingly under attack from left-wing education authorities and others for alleged 'racism', 'sexism', 'imperialism', 'elitism', and much else besides. Many have left the profession.

One result of this has been a dramatic fall in the amount of history actually taught in schools, to the point where the Historical Association is seriously worried. Another result has been a tendency for the character of history teaching itself to change: the teaching of history has been influenced by the current educational fashion for imparting skills rather than knowledge, and also by the fashion for so-called 'child-centred learning'. These changes must also be set against the extremely strong current of egalitarianism running through our education system at all levels.

From all these pressures there emerged in 1976 a 'new philosophy'[2] for the teaching of history which became embodied in the 'Schools Council History (13-16 Project)' (SCHP). Its detractors call it the 'Sacred Cow History Project'[3] – not without reason.

The 'new philosophy' holds that, since nothing is ultimately knowable, and the historical record is selective, subjective and inevitably biased, the actual historical *content* of history is almost valueless. Thus the main benefit from the study of history is the acquisition of certain skills and concepts. The 'skills' in question are those needed 'to interpret and evaluate a wide range of historical sources and their use as evidence' (quoted from the Assessment Objectives of the Midland Examining Group SHP syllabus) and the 'concepts' are those of 'cause and consequence, change and continuity, similarity and difference'.

The SCHP was embodied in a syllabus which has been available in the London area for ten years and has been taken by many thousands of children. It has built up an enthusiastic, one could say fanatical, following among teachers. Its main attraction seems to be that it is aimed at the whole ability range. Since the historical content has been reduced to a minimum it has proved to be acceptable to even the silliest authorities, and this is clearly regarded as a point in its favour. I will describe it in more detail later.

In 1986 Sir Keith Joseph bowed to pressure from the egalitarian lobby and from the secretaries of the teachers' unions and agreed to phase out O-Levels and CSE in favour of the GCSE. What was now required was a new set of history syllabuses aimed at the full ability range. Although it would have been possible to adapt the traditional syllabuses and exams for the purpose there were powerful reasons against doing this. Firstly, there was the regrettable fact that by this time schools had become political battlegrounds. This raised the spectre of endless warfare over the content and slant of the history to be taught. Secondly, there was the very powerful 'anti-racist' lobby whereby anything tending towards integration of the ethnic minorities was condemned as 'racist'. Thirdly, there was the fact of the SCHP phenomenon with ten years' experience and a considerable current of teacher-stridency behind it.

So it came about that the DES turned its back on traditional history teaching and gratefully embraced the 'new philosophy'. The SCHP format clearly offered a very acceptable escape-route from all the difficulties associated with traditional attitudes towards the teaching of history. It also has the almost irresistible attraction of being new, and therefore presumably at the leading edge of new technology. Having announced this exciting new development, Sir Keith resigned, leaving his successor holding a very strange-looking baby.

What the DES did was to incorporate SCHP (now renamed SHP) almost unchanged as one of the optional syllabuses, and to specify that the other syllabuses on offer should follow the SHP philosophy and incorporate its characteristic features. These features are :
(1) An emphasis on the 'skill' of source-evaluation;
(2) A downgrading of historical content;
(3) An emphasis on the designated 'concepts';
(4) A fragmented and topic-based approach;
(5) A substantial element of teacher-assessed coursework.

At this point it is worth noting what has been lost. Firstly, there is the loss of a huge slice of our national heritage. There is no feeling in these new syllabuses that we are talking about our own history. It is always referred to impersonally as 'the past'. This does not apply, however, to the Welsh Joint Education Committee Syllabus, which robustly aims 'to promote an awareness of our (presumably Welsh) national heritage,[4] and it is clear from the syllabus and the test papers that the Welsh Committee means what it says.

There is nothing in the Aims of the Examining Boards in England which might suggest a desire to promote an awareness of our English national heritage. The nearest we get to it is Aim No.4 of the Midland Examining Group SHP which is to 'help pupils, particularly in the sections of the course on British History, towards an understanding of the development over time of social and cultural values'.

I wrote to the Secondary Examinations Council, the body ultimately responsible for all this, and asked what Aim No.4 actually means. I pointed out that it is open to several different interpretations. The Principal Professional Officer replied saying that Aim No.4 does indeed permit a 'range of interpretations', so 'you must ask MEG for their particular interpretation.' In other words they have approved an important pronouncement by a subsidiary body without really knowing, or apparently much caring, what it means. This seems to me a good illustration of the mental and moral cowardice which pervades whole sections of our intellectual establishment.

The second thing which is lost is any attempt to give children any real understanding of our institutions and perennial problems. This is surely a grave error; boys and girls of 14 are within four years of getting the vote. We should be trying to give them some idea of what this means.

The third loss is the life and colour of history. Children like to learn about people. The new philosophy behind the GCSE lets them down.

The fourth loss is the acquisition of a broad perspective which traditional methods of teaching history tried to encourage. This disappears in the new fragmentary, topic-based approach.

The fifth, and possibly most important loss of all, is the rigour and integrity of the subject. The pursuit of truth has been traded for something of very dubious validity. These points may be illustrated by a brief description of some of the syllabuses themselves.

The whole range of GCSE history syllabuses is wide and very confusing. For instance, the Northern Examining Association offers six different syllabuses, all qualified as history. Some syllabuses are not yet available. Some are available but not yet approved by the SEC. All the syllabuses offer a fragmented mixture of choices. It might be supposed that the absurdly wide range of choice would be of benefit to the pupils. In fact the choices are made by the schools to suit their own convenience and preferences. The pupils have to accept the school's choice or drop history altogether. Since all these syllabuses are primarily concerned with source-evaluation, and since this entails the enormous expense of getting tooled-up with all the necessary material for a particular course, it obviously means that once a school is equipped for a certain course it will be extremely reluctant to change, however unsatisfactory the course might turn out to be.

The Midland Examining Group has managed to get all four of its history syllabuses approved by the SEC. They are as follows:

History (British and European History)
History (British Social and Economic History)
History (The Modern World, 1914 to the Present Day)
History (Schools History Project).
The SHP is the one which sets the pattern for the others. It

will be worthwhile therefore to describe it in some detail.

The examination for the SHP consists of two papers, the first taking two hours and taking 30% of the total marks. The second lasts one and a half hours, also taking 30% of the marks. Finally there is the all-important element of coursework, which in this case takes 40% of the total marks.

Paper 2 is the simplest. 'This paper will consist of several compulsory questions (not less than six, and not more than nine) set on a range of source material. The source material may be chosen from any period or type of history, and no prior knowledge of the subject matter of the source material will be required' (quoted from the syllabus). Clearly this is a straight test of the so-called 'skill' of source evaluation. I should perhaps say here that this type of paper seems to be peculiar to the SHP syllabuses.

Paper 1 is split between Section A, which is devoted to what is called a Study in Development (either Medicine Through Time, or Energy Through Time), and Section B which is devoted to what is called a Study in Depth (either Elizabethan England, or Britain 1815-1851, or The American West).

These syllabuses are characterised by a sort of elephantine pretentiousness of Orwellian proportions. Things which the ordinary teenager might be expected to have absorbed quite unknowingly many years previously are pulled out of a hat and endowed with a cosmic significance. Thus it is felt necessary to put these pupils through two years of grappling with Medicine Through Time primarily in order to enable them to acquire a grasp of the concepts of Continuity and Causation. Here it is in black and white:

Continuity
Candidates should appreciate that:

a) old ideas and old techniques continue in use in some areas long after they have been superseded in others;
b) old and new ideas and techniques often continue side by side in the same place.

Similar injunctions are made about the relevance of Causation.

The section concerned with Studies in Depth is preceded by an Introduction consisting of six paragraphs of pretentious nonsense, of which the following extract may suffice as a sample:

Since empathetic understanding is a vital enabling factor in the general historical understanding of any period in the past, the most important objective for the Studies in Depth is an empathetic understanding of the values and beliefs of the time, related to individuals and situations.

The SHP syllabus also contains a very impressive list of Assessment Objectives, and a remarkable table which shows exactly which Assessment Objectives are supposed to be aimed at by the different parts of the exam. It all looks very impressive, not to say frightening, until you look at the Specimen Question Papers. Here we find the reality lurking behind all the long words and infinitely confusing cross-references. After two years of struggling with no less than 31 aspects of (say) Elizabethan England the pupils would typically be confronted with:
Source A – a photocopied portrait of Drake looking bold as brass;
Source B – a quotation from an obscure Spaniard who describes Drake as a firm but fair leader who consults his crew before making any decisions and pays on the nail; and
Source C – a quotation from another Spaniard who reports that Drake has 'at night captured another ship .... bound for

Panama', and lists its cargo.

There is no indication of whether Source B is based on personal acquaintance or mere hearsay.

The pupils then answer the following questions:

(a) Look carefully at Sources A and B.
How do sources A and B help us to understand Sir Francis Drake's success as a sea-captain?
(b) In what ways can Source C be used to criticise Drake?
(c) Would people in the 16th century have seen Drake as a pirate or a hero? Use sources A, B and C and your own knowledge to help you to explain your answer.

In the actual exam there would be two questions of this type, from which the pupil chooses one. Time allowed: 45 minutes.

Whether a single question of this sort is sufficient to elicit the sort of response on which to make a fair judgement of the results of two years' work seems questionable, to say the least. Similar considerations apply to the Specimen Questions on Medicine Through Time. (At present there are no specimen questions available for Energy Through Time.)

The Coursework element is a major commitment. Pupils are expected to submit between four and seven pieces of work over the two years. They are split between some topic of Modern World Studies, of which seven are suggested (e.g. China in the Modern World), and some topic of History Around Us, (e.g. Roman Britain). There are very elaborate instructions to the teacher about how all this is to be organised. Five pages of fine print are devoted to 'The Objectives: Some Guidelines for Setting Assignments'. Objective No. 1 is, of course, 'Evaluation and Interpretation of Sources'. It is certainly not a soft option for the teacher.

In fairness it should be said that the other syllabuses

devised by the Midland Examining Group are somewhat less preoccupied with source-evaluation. In some, the coursework component only covers 20% or 30% of the total marks. Even so, any school wishing to carry on as nearly as possible with the traditional approach to history will certainly have to make major changes and compromises.

With source-evaluation playing such an important role in these syllabuses, overshadowing everything else, including the historical content, it is worth raising several important questions. Is source-evaluation really a 'skill'? Is it something of value outside the historical context? Does it encourage pupils to think for themselves? Even assuming that the answer to each of the above questions is 'yes', is source-evaluation over-valued in these syllabuses at the expense of other things perhaps just as important? My own opinion is that the answers to these questions are by no means clear from the evidence which is available, and there should be an urgent and realistic investigation by independent people.

Source-evaluation is obviously something which professional historians practice, and no doubt some of them are more skilful at it than others. But whether it can be regarded as a readily-acquired 'skill' like riding a bicycle seems extremely doubtful. It depends primarily on knowledge and judgement. But in these syllabuses knowledge is regarded as of secondary importance. For instance, 'it must be emphasised that the acquisition of factual knowledge should not be seen as an end in itself' (quoted from the Midland Examining Group's SHP, page 7).

Whether it encourages pupils to think for themselves and has value outside the historical context is arguable. What seems to me beyond doubt is that seeing history primarily and almost exclusively through source-material distorts and diminishes it. I will take just one example.

In the Midland Group's British Social and Economic
History syllabus Specimen Question Papers, pages 10 and
11, we are dealing with the extremely interesting subject of
universal compulsory education. Among the sources William Cobbett is quoted as objecting to 'taxing the industrious shoemaker in order to make him pay for the education
of the shoemaker who is not industrious', and he goes on to
say that the proposal would 'of necessity create a new and
most terrific control in the hands of the government'. Lord
Chancellor Brougham is quoted as saying that 'If the people
of England were forced to educate their children by
penalties, education would be made absolutely hateful in
their eyes and would speedily cease to be tolerated.' These
are very interesting observations giving plenty of food for
thought. But the questions set by the examiners concentrate
almost exclusively on the sources as *sources*. Only one
sub-question, offering 3 marks out of 30 for all six
questions, touches on the issues raised. This is question 4:
(a) 'Choose ONE criticism of ideas for the education of the
poor from EACH of the sources. Explain what is meant by
EACH of the criticisms.' This can hardly be described as
encouraging the pupils to think for themselves, except on a
very low interpretation of those words. I would say that this
and any number of similar examples prove the point that
source-evaluation on this scale distorts and diminishes
history. It is also very much part of the levelling-down
process already noted in Jonathan Worthen's essay on
English in this volume.

A study of the questions set in these specimen papers and
the 'marking guidance' at the back of the booklet is a very
revealing exercise. It has left me in no doubt that anybody
who wants to get the top marks will have to make a
thorough study of the sort of answers the examiners are
likely to be looking for, however silly they may appear to be

on ordinary commonsense grounds. I have tried some of these questions on graduates among my friends and relations, and their scores would have been abysmal.

Clearly, the teacher is going to have to spend a lot of time habituating the pupils to shaping their answers to fit the models. For instance, a lot of questions take roughly the following form, 'Would Source A be more use to a historian than Source B?' Most often the honest answer would have to be that since both sources have been lifted clean out of their contexts (as for instance 'Speech made in Cardiff during the General Election campaign of 1950'[5] without saying by whom) it is simply not possible to arrive at a fair evaluation of either of them. But this would obviously earn few marks. To answer simply, 'Yes', is equally unlikely to hit the jackpot. But a clever teacher will have drilled his pupils to answer such questions in a more sophisticated manner, irrespective of any knowledge or interest in the subject, for example, 'Source A might be more use as confirmation of the facts, but Source B throws light on what people thought at the time.' Whether this sort of thing can be described as cultivating 'skills', or as 'developing strategies designed simply for the purpose of producing good examining marks' (quoted from a DES letter to me) or both, is a fine point. Others might regard the whole exercise as little better than a parlour game.

As well as the need to cultivate certain skills, the importance of acquiring certain concepts is emphasised in these syllabuses. This is so for no very obvious reason, unless it be simply another way of burying the historical content. Why should 'Continuity' be regarded as of crucial significance, but 'Discontinuity' be totally neglected? 'Causation' is an enormously delicate and complicated business in the historical context. 'Motivation' is surely something about which wise men refrain from pontificating.

'Similarity' and 'Difference'are not some exciting new discovery. A baby can spot both the similarity and the difference between its mother and its aunt long before being able to sit up.

In these syllabuses a great deal of play is made with the words 'empathetic understanding'. Obviously empathetic understanding is a desirable quality to develop, but without knowledge it is nothing more than generalised sentimentality. The GCSE is hardly very sensible in encouraging empathetic understanding while failing to encourage knowledge. It might also be said that GCSE history seems in a terrible hurry to be sympathetic towards everybody else's predicament before ensuring that we have a clear idea of our own standpoint. Here is a recommended 'Typical Empathetic Exercise (10 marks)' from the Welsh Joint Examining Committee: 'Write an article from the point of view of a supporter of President Castro living in Havana in 1962, explaining the missile crisis and condemning American policy in the earlier Bay of Pigs episode.' Is this balanced by another question saying, 'Imagine what it must have been like to be one of the forty million Russians massacred by Lenin and Stalin'? No, it is not.

A strong commitment to coursework in any examination will inevitably raise questions as to the possibility of fair and objective assessment. This is no less true in the case of history than in any other subject. Since the teacher is present at all times while the assignment is being devised, planned, executed and assessed it is impossible to disentangle the input of the teacher from the input of the pupil. Midland Examining Group's SHP syllabus admits that 'The single most important factor influencing candidates' performance in their coursework is the nature of the assignments they are set' (page 17). This surely places an unfair responsibility on the teachers. It would have to be a strange sort of teacher who could stand by and watch a pupil making a terrible hash of his coursework without being tempted to persuade him to change it, and of course, since the pupil would be aware that it would be the teacher who was to mark it, he would have to change it even if he strongly, and perhaps reasonably, disagreed with the teacher's reasoning.

Coursework must be seen as a logical extension of 'child-centred learning'. Although it may well prove to be just one more ephemeral fashion the whole exercise, as applied to history at the present time, is shot through with make-believe. The pupils are not 'finding things out for themselves'. All the source material will have been pre-selected and probably processed in order to make it intelligible. At the very least it is all enormously extravagant of time and resources in relation to what is actually learned.

GCSE history enshrines ideals and assumptions which will inevitably tend to cut us off from our own history. As a result, our self-understanding will be diminished enormously. But the philosophy lying behind the new approach has been introduced without any regard for what the general public actually wants for its children. In criticising the new system, however, I am not advocating the return to some mythical golden age, still less am I in favour of any kind of narrow nationalism. But GCSE history as it stands at the present time can hardly be said to enshrine the best historical education which our children could receive. One step towards remedying the situation before it degenerates still further would be to support the idea of a compulsory core of British history at secondary level, as suggested by the Historical Association. One can only hope that the politicisation of education will not prevent this idea from taking root.

3. MATHEMATICS

Colin Coldman & Ken Shepherd

The introduction of the GCSE examination in mathematics does not, as its supporters (and some critics) claim, signal a major departure from the way the subject is taught in schools. Instead it must be seen as the latest stage in a disastrous process that has seen school mathematics drift towards becoming a low-level empirical science. Obsessed with its utility, and paying no attention to the nature of mathematics as a body of knowledge, the instigators and supporters of this process have, no doubt unwittingly, produced a crisis in mathematics teaching. This crisis is far worse than the problems which beset school mathematics before the 1960s to which the move away from an abstract approach to the subject is a reaction.

The drift away from rigour is likely to continue. The *Times Educational Supplement* (March 6th 1987) carried an article calling for A-level examinations to be made easier. The argument given was that this would lead to more passes and hence to higher standards!

The process of decline has consisted of three clear stages:
(1) the gradual intrusion and acceptance of empirical methodology into the curriculum;
(2) the official legitimation of such methods by the Cockroft Report and the subsequent HMI document;
(3) the institutionalising of the empirical approach with the GCSE examination.

In this essay we trace the history of this development

from the influential work of Bruner[1] and Skemp[2] through to the Cockroft Report and the new GCSE exam. Before doing this, however, it is necessary to establish our argument that it is illegitimate to treat the propositions of mathematics as being empirically verifiable. A brief excursion into the philosophy of mathematics will show that this is so.

Anyone reading the literature in mathematics education could be forgiven for believing the false proposition that there is general agreement about the existence of an empirical basis for mathematics. To quote just one highly significant example, the new London and East Anglian Examining Group (LEAG) alleges that 'There is an irrefutable case to be made in offering pupils an adequate experimental basis and opportunities to be creative within mathematics' (p.7).[3]

In fact almost the opposite is the case. Not since J.S. Mill has any notable philosopher advocated that mathematics is an empirical science. Despite frequent assertions that practical reasoning in mathematics is not only valid but essential, nowhere in the LEAG document (or for that matter any other work advocating an empirical approach) is this view about the nature of mathematics defended.

Mill's philosophy of mathematics is tailor-made as a justification of the teaching methods necessary for GCSE mathematics. It has the advantage of being in line with a commonsense view of the subject, but it is relatively easy to show that it quickly leads to absurdities. In *The Foundations Of Arithmetic*,[4] Frege made a devastating attack on Mill's views on mathematics.

For Mill, numbers are abstractions from sense impressions. Thus the number five is known through consideration of collections of five objects. The laws of arithmetic are also empirically established. $2+1=3$ is a generalisation of the fact that three pebbles can be arranged into two groups containing two pebbles and one pebble. If the statements of mathematics are known any more certainly than those of other sciences, it is only because they are more easily verifiable. They are still generalisations of the laws of nature.

For small numbers, Mill's system may appear to work, but Frege highlights its shortcomings. Noting Mill's method of showing that $2+1=3$, he comments:

> What a mercy, then, that not everything in the world is nailed down; for if it were, we should not be able to bring off this separation, and $2+1$ would not be 3!(p.9).

Frege goes on to ask what physical fact could the number 0 reflect? If the number 3 is an abstraction of all physical aggregates of three objects, Frege notes a further problem:

> From this we can see that it is really incorrect to speak of three strokes when the clock strikes three, or to call sweet, sour and bitter three sensations of taste; and equally unwarrantable is the expression 'three methods of solving an equation'. For none of these is a parcel which ever impresses the senses thus, o⁰o (pp.9-10).

From here on the problems multiply. To take a random large number, 2,687,569,683,830,002 can easily be generated from small numbers through the ordinary laws of arithmetic. But is there any such collection in the universe? If so, how could we recognise it as such and see that it can be divided up in the way Mill's philosophy demands?

> If the definition of each individual number did really assert a special physical fact, then we should never be able to sufficiently admire, for his knowledge of nature, a man who calculates with nine-figure numbers (p.10).

Mill's system of arithmetic creates enough problems with natural numbers (1, 2, 3 ...). It cannot conceivably generate other types of numbers. It can be seen that if a parcel of two objects is halved then the result is a parcel of two. If this in turn is halved then one object is left. We might generously concede then that 4 halved is 2, and 2 halved is 1. Suppose though that the remaining object is halved, then we are left (assuming this is possible) with a parcel of two objects. Should it be concluded then that a half of 1 is 2?

The following quote from Frege can easily be directed at the authors of the LEAG document, or any of the other writers in mathematics education who reduce mathematics to trivial physical facts:

> What, then, are we to say of those who, instead of advancing this work where it is not yet completed, despise it, and betake themselves to the nursery, or bury themselves in the remotest conceivable periods of human evolution, there to discover like John Stuart Mill, some gingerbread or pebble arithmetic! It remains only to ascribe to the flavour of the bread some special meaning for the concept of number. A procedure like this is surely the very reverse of rational, and as unmathematical, at any rate, as it could well be. No wonder the mathematicians turn their backs on it! (Introduction p.7).

Frege pinpoints the error that underlies the whole of Mill's theory:

> Mill always confuses the applications that can be made of an arithmetical proposition which often are physical and do presuppose observed facts, which the pure mathematical proposition itself (p.13).

Exactly the same mistake is made by those writers who are shaping mathematics education in schools. They, unlike

Mill, have not got the excuse that the foundations of mathematics have not received much attention.

The arguments above should not be seen as an attack on empiricism in general, only in mathematics. There are and have been, of course, many mathematicians who would defend empiricism. They have, however, always adopted some form of formalism in mathematics. This treats mathematics as a formal system, regulated by the rules of logic. This, effectively, solves the problems outlined above by divorcing mathematics from reality. The natural number system is re-defined and the certainty of the existence of large positive integers is written into this definition. The existence of such large numbers brings with it no ontological commitment, but exist in the sense that they follow as logical consequences of the definition of natural numbers.

Re-defining the number system not only saves mathematics from uncertainty and ambiguity but also makes it infinitely more powerful. From the natural numbers, other number systems follow as logical constructions. A mathematics limited to sense experience could have no conception of, say, complex numbers, yet these have proved to have uses in physics.

What is true for number theory also holds for geometry. Treating geometry formally has led to the establishment of non-Euclidean geometries, which are often better than a Euclidean model for solving physical spatial problems. Again a naive empirical approach could not have established such geometries.

An objection sometimes made against formalism is that it reduces mathematics to a set of tautologies. This is true, but a tautology should not be confused with a truism. Many of the results of mathematics are surprising but are still logical consequences of definitions. It is this ability to reveal surprising consequences that makes mathematics powerful.

To say that a mathematical statement is a tautology is not to say that it is a *mere* tautology.

There are of course other philosophical accounts of mathematics, chiefly ones which seek to show that the subject matter of mathematical study has an objective existence and comes to be known through intuition. These, however, do not have the same sort of implications for the day-to-day practice of mathematics that Mill's system would have. It is not our intention here to argue for some sort of formalism but simply to identify it as the alternative to Mill's philosophy which empiricists can adopt. This is important because the writers whose work we are about to look at are clearly empiricists who take the naive empiricist view of mathematics. They fail to heed Frege's warning and confuse mathematics with its applications. This, as we shall now argue, has serious consequences when considered in relation to school mathematics.

The Move Away From Rigour

The purpose of the above argument is to expose the poverty of empirical method in mathematics. Having done this, it will be clearer why the way in which the mathematics curriculum has been developed in recent years is of such concern.

The gradual drift away from rigour began as the influence of the work of the American educationist, Bruner, grew. We are not suggesting that all the problems in the way mathematics is taught can be attributed to Bruner, but his work fitted in well with the intellectual mood of the 1960s, and was easily and uncritically assimilated by educationists keen for radical change. Because we are critical of many of his assertions, it should be stressed that some of the reforms in the curriculum that have followed from Bruner's work have been beneficial. The problem has been that because of the blind adherence he has attracted from those that today make up the educational establishment, his theories have not been subject to critical assessment. In other words they have not been allowed to go through the process of natural selection which would sort the good from the bad.

The following passage from Bruner is perhaps the one most frequently quoted and is a fair indication of his outlook on education. It has been overlooked, however, that, for all the optimism contained within it, it is none the less a dogma, and a reckless one at that:

> We begin with the hypothesis that any subject can be taught effectively in some intellectually honest form to any child at any stage of development. It is a bold hypothesis and an essential one in thinking about the nature of the curriculum. No evidence exists to contradict it; considerable evidence is being amassed to support it (Bruner, p.33).

What Bruner fails to mention is that no evidence *could* possibly contradict it, since any successful teaching strategy can be cited as supporting evidence, while unsuccessful methods can be dismissed as not of the right form. It is an implicit assumption that the hypothesis is true and that it simply remains to find the right pedagogical method to communicate any concept to any child. In short the statement is, in Popper's language, unfalsifiable.

One result of Bruner's influence is that primary school teachers, despite the fact that most have no advanced specialist knowledge, have been taught at college to believe the false proposition that they are capable of teaching mathematics and that the children they teach are all capable of learning it. We do not blame the teachers for this; many openly admit that mathematics is not a subject they feel comfortable with. The fault clearly lies with the training colleges for inculcating the view that primary school children not only can but ought to learn advanced mathematical concepts. The damage this has done cannot be understated. To take just one example, many pupils arrive at secondary school, often virtually innumerate, with such a distorted understanding of set theory (the foundation of mathematics) that it is extremely difficult to undo the damage.

Although Bruner was mainly concerned with children of primary age, his influence has gradually permeated the secondary curriculum to the point where the writings of his followers are quoted in support of a practical approach to the GCSE course. Zelda Isaacson, for example, writes in *Teaching GCSE Mathematics*:

> The case for practical work in mathematics ... has been made so thoroughly in so many publications and over so many years that it is not necessary to go through all the arguments again in this book. Every mathematics student has met the work and ideas of, for example, Piaget, Dienes and Bruner, and is aware that most learners need practical experiences in order to make sense of fundamental mathematical concepts and make these their own (p.70).[5]

Several points need to be made here. First, it is strange to quote the work of Piaget alongside Bruner and Dienes as their work is largely oppositional to that of Piaget. Piaget supports the belief that, certainly at the age of 14 and over, mathematics should be taught formally. Second, Isaacson wriggles out of the need to justify her claim by conveniently saying that it has been done elsewhere. This is the same trick that was pulled by LEAG (see above) and the claim is untrue. Apart from the psychological studies done, there is no philosophical attempt to justify the inclusion of practical work, and it is about time that the defenders of such methods faced up to this fact.

Finally, and most importantly, Isaacson has confused mathematics with its applications. Of course learners need to explore physical space before abstract notions of space can be developed. But this is not a *mathematical* experience any more than a child's learning of the meaning of the words 'truth' and 'falsehood' are logical experiences. All Isaacson has done is drawn our attention to the truism that before mathematics can be learned, some concepts must have been formed. But to identify these necessary preconditions for learning mathematics, with mathematical concepts themselves is a gross error, albeit one that is written into the national criteria for GCSE. The error leads to the belief, widely held and again an integral part of the GCSE, that these physical experiences can be substituted for mathematics. Again, this belief originates with Bruner:

> ... it seems highly arbitrary and very likely incorrect to delay the teaching of Euclidean or metric geometry until the end of the primary grades ... *provided that they are divorced from their mathematical expression and studied through materials that the child can handle himself* (Bruner p.43, original emphasis).

This leaves no doubt as to Bruner's view of geometry. It is a description of physical space, and as such can be known through sense experience. Thus the normal reason for studying geometry is unceremoniously stood on its head. Instead of Euclidean geometry being a logically self-contained system that can be used to model the world with some success, it becomes the end result of physical experiment.

Richard Skemp, the mathematician turned psychologist, is another writer whose work has clearly influenced the mathematics curriculum. He at least has a more sophisticated conception of mathematics as evidenced by his statement that 'Mathematics cannot be learnt directly from the everyday environment' (p.32).

However, Skemp goes on to draw a very curious conclusion from this – one that leads him to ignore his own observation:

> ... this makes him (the learner) largely dependent on his teachers (including all who write mathematical textbooks); and, at worst, it exposes him to the possibility of acquiring a lifelong fear and dislike of mathematics (p.32).

The first assertion here is obviously true for all subjects, the second simply does not follow from the premise. Why should the fact that mathematics has a logical structure lead to people fearing it? If anything, its unshakeable truths should lead to a feeling of security. Of course some will inevitably come to dislike it, as is the case with any subject. There is, after all, no accounting for taste. A far more likely source of pupil discontent in mathematics is the premature exposure to its complexities and the way a challenging, difficult subject is trivialised by constant reference to practical experience.

Skemp's view leads him to overestimate the psychological barriers to learning mathematics. This in itself is not too serious but he uses this as a justification for abandoning a logical approach to mathematics. He creates a false conflict between mathematics as a body of knowledge and the psychological state of mathematical understanding. This confusion is both typical of, and integral to, later developments which have resulted in the GCSE syllabus. Thus, in commenting on the presentation of mathematics as a logical system, he states that:

This approach is laudable in that it aims to show that mathematics is sensible and not arbitrary, but is mistaken in two ways. First, it confuses the logical and psychological approaches. The main purpose of a logical presentation is to convince doubters; that of a psychological one is to bring about understanding (p.13).

The claim that the purpose of a logical presentation is to convince doubters is surely misleading. This may occasionally be the case but the principal reason for employing such a presentation is to make manifest the consequences of adopting certain definitions. Whatever form a psychological presentation consists in, it is clear that it stands in the way of a logical development of mathematics. Even if the psychological presentation makes the learning process easier, it cannot justify such an exposition if adopting it distorts what is to be taught. The very nature of the subject demands a logical exposition.

Skemp goes on to make dubious claims about what mathematical thinking consists in, when he states that a logical presentation of mathematics gives:

only the end-product of mathematical discovery ... and fails to bring about in the learner those processes by which mathematical discoveries are made. It teaches mathematical thought, not mathematical thinking (p.13).

Skemp's first assumption is simply false. A logical development shows the link between initial definitions and final discovery. Of all subjects, mathematics is the one that reveals most about the processes that lead to conclusions. It is also disingenuous of Skemp not to acknowledge that a logical presentation can be supplemented by other teaching methods.

The second of Skemp's assertions reveals more of what

he is really getting at. Teachers should not so much teach mathematics as teach mathematical thinking. But it is a fundamental mistake to assume that we have to choose between the two. Skemp clearly does not consider it enough for the learner to show that he knows by his performance. If it is *real* understanding it must be accompanied by a particular mental state. Skemp's whole book suffers from being locked into the language of the Cartesian model of mind. He talks, to take just one example, of forming concepts in the mind of the learner (p.32). He presupposes the unlikely and unnecessary hypothesis that mathematical activity must be guided by a particular type of mental activity. He goes on to construct a whole network of concepts which only serve to deflect attention away from the teaching of mathematics, for example: 'To understand something means to assimilate it into an appropriate schema' (p.46).

We assert that we can infer someone understands a piece of mathematics from his ability to derive the result, if appropriate, and apply it as necessary. Teaching mathematics has always implicitly taught mathematical thinking. Concentrating as Skemp does on the mental processes involved distracts us away from the logic of mathematical discovery.

The Cockroft Report

The Cockroft Report, *Mathematics Counts*,[6] was commissioned with good reason. Despite the drift away from rigour, the level of attainment in mathematics continued to remain low. The Report had a golden opportunity to reverse the decline in the transmission of mathematics in school – it failed miserably. Astonishingly it commented on the low general level of mathematical ability amongst the population, yet recommended the continuation of the methods that have accompanied this decline. The Cockroft Report was followed by a detailed statement of aims and objectives from HMI which encompassed the findings of Cockroft. This marks a crucial stage in the decline in rigour in mathematics, as official approval could now be claimed for a non-abstract approach to teaching mathematics.

The opening chapter of the Report is entitled 'Why Teach Mathematics?' This should have been the most important question asked by the committee, suggesting a thorough examination of the structure of the subject and its importance within society. Instead, the reader is confronted with the same old hackneyed phrases about its usefulness and it being 'a powerful tool'. Above all it is a powerful means of communication – a nice phrase but Cockroft is not very clear about what this means. Only that this is the 'principal reason for teaching mathematics to all children' (p.1). What is not discussed is the fact that the power of mathematics lies in its method of tautological transformation which reveals the consequences of its definitions. It is only because of this aspect of mathematics that it is so useful as a modelling system, which so impresses the Cockroft committee. Of course an investigation along these lines would have indicated the need for a logical development of mathematics.

Cockroft, however, is dismissive of the idea that mathematics should be taught because of its inherent logical structure:

> It is often suggested that mathematics should be studied in order to develop powers of logical thinking, accuracy and spatial awareness. The study of mathematics can certainly contribute to these ends but the extent to which it does so depends on the way mathematics is taught (p.2).

Early in the Report, then, it is suggested that a non-abstract approach may be valid. Later we see that not only is an empirical approach approved but is seen as essential:

> It is too often assumed that the need for practical activity ceases at the secondary stage, but this is not the case. Nor is it the case that practical activity is needed only by those pupils whose attainment is low; pupils of all levels of attainment can benefit from the opportunity for appropriate practical experience (pp.72-73).

This is a typical passage from Cockroft, stating that something is the case but offering no supporting evidence or argument, merely handing down judgement from on high. If Hume's famous dictum were to apply, then the Report would certainly be committed to flames. Unfortunately its influence is such that it cannot be so easily dismissed.

Another crucial problem, one that is at the heart of the crisis in mathematics teaching, is the distinction between numeracy and mathematics. A proper distinction between the two would allow the essential numerical skills of life to be taught by any effective method. This would allow mathematics to be taught as it should be – with due respect for its structure. This simple distinction between mathematics and numeracy would go some way to alleviating the problems which faced the committee (but which it deliberately understressed). Since numeracy would not necessarily require a mathematics specialist, this would release teachers to teach the subject they trained in. This may also attract more mathematicians into teaching (although it would have to be accompanied with realistic salary levels). Something of this sort is certainly required, as the figures contained in the Cockroft Report pertaining to the shortage of mathematics specialists are a national disgrace. Page 258 of the

Report reveals that in a survey of secondary schools it was found that only one-third of mathematics teachers had 'good' qualifications in the subject. Even this figure included teachers who only studied mathematics as a subsidiary subject but studied a 'related' subject as their main area of study.

Cockroft, however, is too concerned with supporting the new orthodoxy of practical mathematics to worry about such problems. It ends the discussion on numeracy by failing to distinguish it from mathematics and by saying: 'We are, in fact, asking for more than is included in Collins but not as much as is implied by that in the Oxford dictionary' (p.11). The extraordinary thing is not that such a report could be published, but that it should be so well received and be so influential.

GCSE Mathematics

Much that is contained within the national criteria guide for GCSE mathematics has been strongly influenced by the Cockroft Report. One of its mostly widely quoted passage has impressed itself into the national criteria almost word for word. On page 159 of Cockroft we read that: '...examination papers ... should be such that they enable candidates to demonstrate what they do know rather than what they do not know.' This is mirrored by the requirement of the national criteria that all assessment should: 'enable all candidates to demonstrate what they know, understand and can do'.

These statements are typical of the new orthodoxy. Their superficial appeal hides the full implications of their meanings. All examinations test on the basis of the syllabus, and in this sense test what the candidates know. Presumably something more than this is being said here. If we really are to test only what is known, this presupposes that we know what the candidate knows. This has two consequences: it makes the assessment redundant, and it implies that we have previously assessed the candidate in ignorance of what he knows, for otherwise how could we know what his performance will be?

Since we cannot believe that this is what these statements mean we can only conclude that they are euphemisms for making exams easier. Our belief that this is the intention behind the national criteria is strengthened by the change from norm-referenced to criteria-referenced examinations.

The full extent of the lowering of assessment standards can be seen from the LEAG document. Comment here is superfluous:

> How can we guarantee that work submitted is the pupil's own? In all honesty we cannot.
> ... it is counter-productive to give a low mark such as 5/20. A written comment that reflects the worth of the piece of work relative to the pupil's ability may be more appropriate.
> Help (in assessments) should always be seen as offering leading questions or dropping hints. Pupils should only be told what to do on the rarest occasions (p.14).

The general national criteria also allow Isaacson to state the following:

> ... it points out that as teachers of mathematics we should be aware, and help our pupils become aware, of the many social, political, economic and environmental issues which may be related to mathematical activities (p.12).

This seems to go well beyond what can reasonably be expected of a mathematics teacher and, in the wrong hands, could lead to all kinds of propagandising and indoctrination.

As Isaacson moves on to the subject criteria, the full extent of the damage that is being inflicted on the mathematics curriculum becomes clear. One of the aims of the GCSE course is to: 'develop a feel for number, carry out calculations and understand the significance of the results obtained'.

Isaacson draws out the implications: 'It no longer matters whether people can do long division "by hand"'(p.13). Further on she comments that: 'Learning to use a calculator effectively is much more important than being able to remember and reproduce accurately a complex algorithm'(p.16).

Of course learning to use a calculator is indeed a valuable skill but many would disagree that pupils should not learn long multiplication and division skills. Unfortunately their reasons are often not very good, being of the 'what if the batteries fail?' variety. The reason why these skills should be part of a good mathematics course is much more fundamental. We have already noted that mathematics is a process of tautological transformation, revealing often surprising results. It is not immediately obvious that 31x64=1984, but we need know nothing else than the correct rules for reasoning to quickly establish this fact. The long multiplication process is a convenient way of applying these rules. When a student practices this process, then, he is not wasting his time. Rather he is learning correct rules of mathematical deduction. It is this that above all justifies the place on the curriculum of such methods. They are mini-paradigms of mathematical argument.

Isaacson, however, is apparently no fan of logic:

> We need to combat the belief that mathematics is dry, cold and just about logic, by emphasising that mathematics is also about beauty, elegance, excitement and imagination (p.15).

Are we to conclude then that logic cannot furnish us with elegance or fire our imagination? We would not go so far as to assert that logic has the objective qualities of beauty and excitement but we must remember that many mathematicians were so inspired by the deductive logic of Euclid.

LEAG takes up the same theme:

> The perennial complaint about the teaching of mathematics in schools is that it is too abstract (p.7).

No doubt the complaint levelled against history teaching is that it is all about the past! What boring old logic is to be replaced with, of course, is the excitement of practical mathematics: 'Mathematics should become more reliant on the use of practical aids'(p.9). And Isaacson claims that: 'It has been a source of great frustration for many mathematics teachers that our subject has been seen as theoretical and book-bound rather than practical' (Isaacson p.71).

As has been noted, practical mathematics has been creeping into the curriculum for some time, but with the GCSE it is required of all schools to use such teaching and assessment methods. Presumably, Isaacson and the authors of the LEAG document have all at some time benefited from learning through the formal methods they openly despise. What we cannot understand is why they wish to deny the same opportunities to others. Public schools will surely not abandon formal teaching methods any more than the new examination dictates. Why should bright students in comprehensives be put at an even greater disadvantage? If assignments can be done at home, this can only benefit middle class pupils. The real losers with the new GCSE mathematics examination will be, as usual, bright working class pupils who have an aptitude for mathematics. They will be placed at a disadvantage by informal teaching and assessment methods and held back by the sterility of practical mathematics. Above all they will receive a distorted picture of the subject; the true appeal of mathematics – its logical structure – will be masked by dreary appeals to empirically established laws. They will turn away from a subject that ought to play a major part in their lives.

Conclusions

We have argued at some length that there is no place for empiricism in a mathematics course, and that the structure of mathematics demands a formal exposition. It may be argued that this is an elitist view, as it will inevitably mean that some pupils cannot take such a course. This we readily concede, for it is a fact that mathematics is a difficult subject and, as with anything difficult, it will be beyond the intellectual grasp of some people. What we should on no account do is offer them a third rate practical subject and pretend that this is mathematics simply because it happens to share some of its results. The GCSE examination not only does this, but drags everyone down to the same level and therefore manages to insult the intelligence of both high and low attainers.

The 'maths for all' bandwagon was started by Bruner with his claim that anyone can learn anything. This has been a constant factor running through all the literature and can be seen in the work of Zelda Isaacson and the LEAG document. Isaacson is fond of quoting Lewis Carroll. If she had paid more attention to the following passage, however, she might have realised that she should not be so hasty in concluding that everyone is capable of learning mathematics:

'How am I to get in?' asked Alice again, in a louder tone.
'Are you to get in at all?' said the footman. 'That's the
first question, you know.'
It was no doubt: only Alice did not like to be told so.

The drift away from rigour began as an understandable
reaction to an outdated curriculum. There was, however,
another movement which sought to introduce a rigorous
exposition of modern mathematics. The Cockroft Report
quotes, unfavourably, the aims of the original School
Mathematics Project (SMP). They are worth repeating here
as they give an excellent example of the way school
mathematics could have been developed:

> a major aim of the syllabus is to make school mathematics
> more exciting and more enjoyable, and to impart a
> knowledge of the nature of mathematics and its uses in the
> modern world. In this way, it is hoped to encourage more
> pupils to pursue further the study of mathematics, to bridge
> the gulf which at the moment separates university from
> school mathematics (quoted from Cockroft p.81).

Mathematics has traditionally provided a first class
training in disciplined and exact thinking. The GCSE
system does nothing to uphold and encourage the aims and
values of traditional mathematics teaching. On the contrary, under the GCSE, true mathematics is likely to
disappear from the curriculum altogether to be replaced by
an empirical subject sharing the same name and results, but
not its structure. Frege gave a warning that an empirical
methodology in mathematics should be avoided at all costs.
The same warning can be applied today to the views that
support practical mathematics in opposition to a formal
exposition:

In their own interests mathematicians should, I consider, combat any view of this kind, since it is calculated to lead to the disparagement of a principal object of their study, and of their science along with it. (Frege p.4)

4. MODERN LANGUAGES

Gisela M'Caw

Although in some ways the new GCSE system incorporates many necessary changes in modern language teaching, there is no doubt that we are now presented with a landscape in which there are considerable tracts of land abandoned or conveniently ignored. If we are aware of these defects and resolutely work to maintain if not to improve our standards, then teachers should be able to accept the new examination with a positive outlook. There may still be a danger that the less experienced teacher will misinterpret the new approach, but this might yet be remedied by adjusting teacher training and post-graduate teaching diploma courses. On the other hand, a case could be made for some immediate adaptation of the GCSE by supplementing the new strategy.

One very positive aspect of the GCSE in Modern Languages is to be seen in the emphasis on oral skill: this is given a much higher percentage of the examination result and entails the allocation of more time to each candidate. The various Boards allow as much as fifteen to twenty minutes per pupil at the extended level. Because twenty minutes is a long time for a meaningful dialogue, preparation for it must expand accordingly. The GCSE will work well only if teachers concentrate on oral work as early as possible in the curriculum, so that pupils enjoy the course from the very start. It is obvious that under the new system the teacher's time and energy are of crucial significance, and it would help a great deal if classes can be kept small.

In my own school the new emphasis on oral skill in the curriculum has enabled children to practise dialogue and pronunciation through acting and role-play. Such activities no doubt enable children to appreciate the importance of correct stress and intonation, and as a result, they will be well equipped to deal with the oral aspect of the examination. I must stress, however, that the pupils in my school in their first year of German, had been given a thorough grounding in basic phonology, basic morphological and syntactic patterns, and that they had always practised these in short sentences and always in a meaningful manner. In their textbook every chapter concluded with a dialogue. With the help of this book, dialogue and role-playing became familiar to them. In addition *German* comprehension and translation into English were frequently practised. It is here that my first criticism of the new examination emerges. The GCSE has dropped the requirement for the development of all-round skills, for example translation and German comprehension exercises, during the first year of the course. It is left solely to the individual school and teacher to decide whether to enrich the child's vocabulary through the tried and trusted techniques of translation and comprehension. But *this* is the way to enrich their vocabulary rather than by learning lists of disconnected words. If we are to give children the best opportunities for learning we must not abandon our successful strategies simply because they may not be required in the final examination.

An examination which denigrates or neglects the importance of writing in the target language and comprehending how this language works may be well-intentioned, and may succeed in making things easier for the G, F, E, or even D candidates. But it is extremely unkind, and indeed unfair, to those pupils who expect a C grade or higher, for they will be at a disadvantage later on at A-level, when they find themselves with only the very basic writing skills. The pupil who has gained a C grade at GCSE level may well end his course only with the following meagre 'skills': he can concoct a list of ten items, say of food or clothing or holiday activities; he can write 30 words of information about arrival and departure; and he can give directions to somewhere mentioning which bus or tram to catch. Two Examinations Boards state that for this level of ability 'complete sentences are not required'. But surely, in that case, a C grade GCSE is simply not worth striving for. Nor is it likely that a low-ability pupil *will* strive for this examination: he knows that he does not have to complete his sentences, he need not worry about tenses, verbal conjugation, genders or case-endings. Nothing taxing is required of him – he does not have to ask for 'fresh' eggs or a 'thick' pullover, for example – and, as a result, nothing good will be obtained from him. If only in this respect the GCSE represents a clear example of educational devaluation.

The inadequacy of the GCSE becomes even more apparent when we look at grades B and A (the higher levels in writing, listening and reading comprehension). Most pupils will have to take a large leap in order to cope with the difficult text. In order to reach an A grade, all the training for the basic levels is a waste of time. In such circumstances we might well ask, how can the new system be properly implemented when the teacher is faced with a large class of mixed-ability children? Should the teacher simply aim to instill the basic skills or should he try to teach grammatical pattern and agreement? The extreme disparity between the higher and lower grade levels will create a situation in which some pupils will inevitably be at a disadvantage in mixed-ability classes.

The recommendations of the GCSE for Modern Languages are at best inadequate and at worst utterly destructive of adequate language teaching. No pupil can ever learn to identify language patterns simply through memorising incoherent language fragments, such as shopping lists or hurried messages. Nor will he do so through multiple choice exercises, and even less if he is told from the start that sentences need not be completed.

When a child is taught to use a language naturally and in a meaningful way, the resulting mental alertness fosters and encourages further skill in social communication. This helps his emotional development and strengthens his general motivation. Gradually an attitude becomes established which accepts the grammatical system (the linguistic framework) of that code of communication, but if gaps have been left in the educational strategy or teaching method then that child's progress will have been hindered considerably. Even the less able pupil, accustomed perhaps to the restricted code of communication current in his own home, can eventually grasp the pattern of a second language if he is exposed to it long enough.

We as teachers have a responsibility to our pupils to develop their abilities to the highest level. However, the GCSE does little or nothing towards encouraging teachers to exercise that responsibility.

It is perhaps too early to evaluate the material produced by the various Examination Boards; some adjustments are sure to be made in the near future. Nevertheless, if one compares the data issued so far it can be seen that all the Boards have good and bad points within the three levels which the National Criteria have devised. However, it would appear that the GCSE is biased towards comprehensive education, for little if any account is taken of variants in the level of pupils' intelligence. This very failure to differentiate between the ability and aptitude of the pupils is only too obvious from the fact that they all have to sit the Common Core Basics examination, and indeed this is an important part of the purpose of the whole scheme.

Traditionally there were nine different kinds of language skill that were examined. Not all were equally as important but to reduce the nine skills to four, in all modern languages, as we find in the GCSE, is to adopt a very inadequate and summary approach. We now have four skills but at three different levels of accomplishment – which means twelve papers for the able candidate who wants to go on to study a modern language at A-Level.

It becomes clear that if the mode of examination is to serve also as a model for teaching methods then a great deal of filling-in has to be done by the individual teacher if the pupil is to become a proficient communicator, able to express himself freely and clearly. The teacher will have to add to his own competence in pedagogy some qualifications or experience in upholding all-round standards of fluency.

Recognition and comprehension exercises are important: Gestalt theorists stress the importance of an overview of the whole language as a pre-requisite for any meaningful, intelligent solution to the problem in hand. Whilst an object has a name it is much more important to be aware of the link between the word and the object's inherent quality; this quality the pupil can only discern and apprehend if he himself has used the word, heard it, written it, spoken it and mentally 'located' it. Is it enough, therefore, merely to test just four skills; would the thing, or act, or place really be understood?

The old GCE O-Level offered a more balanced approach than the new GCSE. It tested most of the essential skills to learn a language and it gave the teacher more direction in training the pupil in these skills. Dictation boosted the child's efficiency in spelling; comprehension (with answers stated in the target language) was a step towards written work in other papers. The former practice of listening comprehension, in which the teacher read a passage three times and also divided it into three sections, provided a reasonable as well as an enjoyable test.

In the GCSE, however, there are three listening-comprehension tests, but at the Higher Level Part II the set passage consists of about 200 words which is read only twice (except in the London and East Anglian Group where it is read three times). The LEAG also chooses a somewhat easier vocabulary at Higher Level. In the Midland Examining Group (MEG) the passage is to be read without pauses and without breaking into sections. Other Boards break up the text into two or more sections. In all cases the words are to be heard not from a visible teacher but from a recorded voice. With the MEG , in particular, an enormous jump in ability is expected. It may well be attempted by a few – but even then surely with a measure of frustration. The procedure is unnatural and unbalanced. Normally the listener would be able to interrupt the speaker if he could not follow. There is evidence to show that the pupil's grasp of the content of a passage becomes progressively worse as he goes on listening without a break. He can no longer absorb and decode the sounds he hears. Consequently the passage to be read should not be too long.

The three opportunities for the able candidate to display his skill in listening-comprehension constitute a large part in the examination, but the practice for these papers is a dead end in itself. What the pupil does not know he cannot supply and it is to be noted that his answers at every level are required to be written in English! This affords him no practice (or chance to show competence) in the target language to which he has had to listen. He is wholly passive towards the (unknown) speaker's voice. This procedure is the antithesis of modern language-learning theories which stress the *use* of the language concerned. If the recorded voice in the comprehension test aims primarily at clarity of enunciation there may be little to help the listener with language patterns – often accentuated by intonation and speed. In attending to a recorded voice there is little to suggest an 'encounter' with a person. As a result, the child loses an important chance to gain confidence and he may well become less inclined to persevere towards more advanced studies.

There is also a three-fold test in reading-comprehension. The preparation for this is a much more structural exercise when used as a teaching tool, building up the pupil's confidence, because:

(a) he can work at his own speed;
(b) he receives a visual stimulus;
(c) he recognises language patterns;
(d) he becomes acquainted with idiomatic phrases;
(e) he can recognise the root of some words or a collage of what belongs together, thus enriching his vocabulary.

Some Boards have used pictures of all kinds to facilitate recognition and make the language real and purposeful. As long as any handwritten letters reproduced in the test are legible, this adds to authenticity. If the pupil chooses both comprehension skills at the Higher Level parts 1 and 2, he will then have spent 2 hours doing comprehension work alone.

The Midland Examining Group (MEG) is the least imaginative in prescribing its writing skills papers. There is not one cue in German – not a map, not a picture – and instructions are all in English. The London and East Anglian Group (LEAG) as well as the Northern Examining Association (NEA) both supply pictures and also include a reply-to-a-letter, and a map printed in German with a number of meaningful and relevant questions which must be answered. I notice that all Boards aim at the imperfect tense at the Higher Level, and this, at least, is an excellent feature.

The teacher who wishes to improve upon GCSE recommendations might do well to incorporate the former GCE procedure – the oral reproduction of a story where an outline is given and the passage read twice. While this might be considered to be too hard for some pupils I think that the preparation for it provides an excellent training of the ear for the retention of structures and idioms. It is also a means of testing comprehension, as well as being a teaching device combining listening with a writing skill – whether story or letter or a report. Of course during classwork the story could be broken up as it is being taught and its bare outline could serve as a base for enlargement of vocabulary. Much the same value can be derived from picture-stories, especially if these are linked with the GCSE topics such as travel, school exchanges, food and drink, etc. These topics could suggest several opportunities for most of the skills, not just the oral one. Most of the topics can be used quite early on for various activities. Ideally these activities should be specifically selected so as to find the needs of each individual language.

French, which is treated as the main or sole compulsory modern language in so many schools, cannot be dealt with in exactly the same way as other minority languages such as German, Spanish, Italian or Russian. Whereas one can fully accept that much more time has to be allocated to the systematic teaching of the structure of French sounds so as to develop techniques for its comprehension, German, for example, is very different. It is phonetically easy for the English speaker but morphologically fiendishly difficult:

merely to extend the time spent in listening and in reading – comprehension will not do the trick. In this respect the approach to the language course has to be very different, the more so because these minority-language courses are invariably shorter and more condensed than those provided for French. Given the different needs of each language it seems to be a great waste of time having to concentrate on the Common Core Basics. Teaching methods have to be markedly different in the teaching of, for instance, French, German and Russian, although identical requirements are stipulated for examining them. This is an inappropriate simplification and it leaves many areas uncovered for the teacher and the writers of school textbooks.

The GCSE presents us with the creation of a restricted Common Core and a higher level scheme which neglects much that is of value. There is however another aspect that should give rise to even more concern, *viz.* the new pattern of assessment.

Each pupil has to be graded and labelled before he actually sits the examination. When, with some trepidation, I expressed my anxiety over this procedure to the Board, the reply was that it would be to the pupil's disadvantage if he were put in the wrong grade. Everyone would agree with that remark but *how* is that classification to be determined *before* the examination? There are four sorts of pupil who might be involved at this stage. The GCSE requires us to predict which child falls into which category.

* Pupil 1 offers us no problem. He is able and a reliable worker and steadily follows the teacher's advice and guidance. We can safely predict that he will get an A or B grade.

* Pupil 2 has very limited ability but works hard. Pressures from other subjects prevent him from making a concentrated and consistent effort. He finds it difficult to retain the

new vocabulary and idiomatic expressions, and does not find it easy to grasp language patterns. None the less, with a great deal of repetition and perhaps a short stay in the country of the target language he could in the end do much better than we had thought likely. The teacher hopes for the pupil's moderate success, but it must be admitted that the current educational philosophy is no great help to him. The pupil has to be informed that he cannot take any of the higher level papers because a pass at Common Core Basic level cannot be predicted – thereby deflating his zeal and perseverance. Formerly, when the GCE Awarders sent an analysis of results after O-Level it often showed a considerable discrepancy between unseen translation and comprehension on the one hand and the free composition papers on the other: a pupil could obtain a B-grade based on good results in the former papers because he had been abroad. This is no longer possible with the GCSE because the weaker pupil will not be entered for the higher levels. This serious restriction relating to assessment is curiously alien to the modern view of the importance of communication and comprehension in the foreign language.

* Pupil 3 is lazy. His parents do not bother much about his progress at school and the child remains undisciplined and usually unmotivated. Yet he may not be unintelligent and might produce a surge of last minute effort or ambition. Consequently, to everyone's surprise, he does much better than his teachers thought possible. But in the GCSE system of grading he cannot jump on to the platform for the higher levels because as a result of his previously bad record his teacher is unable to register his name.

* Pupil 4 is the all-rounder: someone who has a place in two or three sports teams and not only plays for the school but may occasionally play for the county. He is out playing sport every Saturday and may also have a part in school

drama or play in the orchestra. A splendid fellow indeed (and I know some) but what about his examinations? Now I am prepared to admit that such a pupil may use the special timetable-freedom before exams to go straight home, pull out all the stops, work at revision, swot the notes and hand-outs he had been given by the teachers – and do this cramming unknown to his teacher. His answers at the time of 'mocks' earlier in the year may have been pretty awful and the staff knew the reasons. But they did not anticipate his determination just before the examination and made no allowance for this. What then? The GCSE grading scheme dims one's pedagogical foresight whereby bridges can be built towards advanced studies and doors approached which could open up far-reaching possibilities for the child. Rigidly to control the development of our pupils, even through careful use of the assessment maintained through-out the preceding year, cannot always ensure that justice is done to those girls and boys who have diligence rather than flair, are late-developers, or are held back by a lack of home encouragement or by unfortunate friendships. Surely it is wrong for teachers prematurely to down-grade those young people who, with effort, might still produce excellent results.

Language is an all-important part of our lives and can be an immensely powerful medium of expression both perso-nally and nationally. It is agreed by all that the purpose behind language education is to enable children to com-municate with other peoples using an additional mode of communication, i.e. that they should have the ability to recognise and use another language adequately. By this means the child can become informed about cultural differences and be equipped to respond wisely to the relevant circumstances of his life. In addition, the GCSE calls for 'authenticity' in the practical use of language.

These intentions are not new. Good teachers have always aimed at imparting such skills. The Nuffield Method brought a quiet revolution into our classrooms, and BBC German courses have consistently emphasised real life patterns. For a long time we have been teaching what was useful and valuable outside the walls of the school. Many teachers take groups of children to foreign countries, where they share for a while the home life and culture of other nations. It can hardly be said that our methods have not been 'authentic' during those GCE years!

But now, with the new GCSE programme, we are drawn away from an open landscape, with its interesting lanes and footpaths, into a restrictive scenery of cuttings and tunnels, with little outlook on either side. It is regrettable that the GCSE system has destroyed much that was imaginative and challenging in modern language teaching. It is now up to the individual teacher to employ his or her educational abilities so as to implement and nurture a natural and wholesome approach to modern languages. This should be done in a constructive way, in order to fill the gaps in GCSE teaching strategies. Only by so doing can we safeguard the standard of our A-Level candidates and continue to pave their way to university excellence.

5. MUSIC

Simon Wyatt

On an initial cursory glance, the new GCSE examination for Music appears quite attractive, with its emancipation of musical styles and teaching methods, and therefore a broadening of the curriculum. The old GCE and CSE syllabuses have been accused in the past of determining, even of stifling, the curriculum. Now with GCSE, some of the unnecessarily unreal academic practices are done away with, and we have at last what purports to be a curriculum-led examination, which can allow for development and innovation, rather than an examination-led curriculum. The importance of composition is now officially recognised by being made an internally-assessed coursework activity, together with the two other components of the examination, Listening and Performing.

If GCSE represented merely a change of approach, or emphasis, however, one would have less cause for concern. 'For most subjects', the Secondary Examinations Council Guide for GCSE Music states, 'the impact of the GCSE Criteria will be principally on how the subject is assessed rather than on the content of the curriculum for that subject. For Music, however, the National Criteria have clear implications not only for how music is assessed, but also for *what* is taught, especially in the later years of secondary schooling.'[1] It is when one examines more closely the National Criteria that the philosophical direction and the educational trends, which are the inspiration behind the new examination, begin to show themselves. One county music advisor has stated recently: '... the National Criteria for Music are amongst the most radical. The changes here as elsewhere are in the direction of downgrading the memorising of facts in favour of skills relevant to an age of rapid change.'[2]

The National Criteria

The aims in the Criteria include concepts of '*developing sensitivity* towards music through *personal experience*', 'the developing of *performing skills*' and 'the *stimulation* and developing of an appreciation and enjoyment of music through an *active* involvement in the three musical activities: listening, performing and composing' (my italics). It seems to me, however, that, as interpreted by the various syllabuses these aims mean in practice that, unless something is readily experienced, it is not valid educationally. The emphasis is on 'intellectual and aesthetic stimulation' rather than on growth or understanding. Thus, for composing, any sort of musical style is acceptable because it springs from the musical experience of the child. The same is true for performing. On the other hand, the formal study of the masterpieces of Western music is relegated to a small percentage of the total examination, and is, in any case, optional. The listening tests too, by their nature, depending on a few initial hearings, demand an immediate response. The approach recognised by the new examination (which has, of course, been around in music education for a number of years) is inevitably child-centred. The role of the teacher is to guide and nurture the musical instincts of the child, whatever they may happen to be. His aim is to deal in concepts rather than to teach.

One specific aim of the new examination is 'to develop a

perceptive, sensitive and critical response to music of
different styles in a cultural and historical context.' A
tendency towards a variety of styles is inevitable in
composition and performance given a broadly-based examination and an ethos that encourages self-expression. In
the Listening component, however, this becomes untenable. 'We must avoid exclusivity' states the SEC guide,
'giving the impression that only a few traditions of music are
acceptable'.[3] Teachers are encouraged to 'an open-minded
acceptance of a variety of musical styles'.[4] The practical
implications for teaching and teacher training loom large.
Such broad-mindedness means in practice a bias towards
music of this century, together with an emphasis on music of
more popular and traditional idioms. The Midland Examining Group (MEG) Syllabus 'A' exemplifies this in its
specimen paper, where only three of the eleven general
extracts are outside these categories. The wisdom of such a
wide exposure for all is to be doubted, especially when it
will operate at the expense of that music which is part of the
foundation of our cultural heritage. Even a university or
college course which aims to study a history of music from
the Renaissance to the present day barely surveys the
period; much less a secondary school course which includes
Eastern, African, Afro-Caribbean and Asian music alongside Western European music of the baroque, classical and
romantic periods. It is not that the study of the music of
other cultures does not have its place, but that the
impracticalities of covering everything will result in superficiality. Although Listening is meant to absorb the formal
analysis of set works, the lives of the composers of those
works and the context of their composition, these are all
treated as of little importance. Indeed in most syllabuses,
they are optional and only then given a 7.5% (MEG
Syllabus 'A', 2 set works) to 10% (London and East

Anglian Group Syllabus, one work) of the total examination. Those in Wales are perhaps the most fortunate with one work for detailed study and a number listed for general study. How one is supposed as a teacher to develop in the children this perceptive and critical response in *any* cultural or historical context is beyond imagination.

Listening

What the Listening component in fact achieves may be gathered by a closer inspection of the specimen papers which accompany the various syllabuses. It is to be examined by means of a gramophone record, and all candidates will answer the written questions on the music, except those not undertaking the set work(s). Most tests are based on previously unheard extracts which are heard up to four times, and the answers required from the candidates must be immediately forthcoming. Where prepared study is necessary in the form of set works, the questions are based on such short extracts (e.g. 17 or 28 bars in MEG Syllabus 'A') that one wonders how much formal preparation is really needed. MEG Syllabus 'A' presents no choice in those set works, something which has in the past allowed both teacher and pupil a certain freedom to pursue particular preferences. (The music set for this first examination is a Smetana overture and four songs from Queen's 'The Works'. I have heard of one parent who has withdrawn a child from the course because of the unsuitability of the words of the latter. Alas, for teachers, there is no such option.) The extracts are, however, printed, so that at least some study of the score is called for in the examination. The extracts in the specimen paper of the Southern Examining Group (SEG) are not printed, and the questions for each of the two set works are based on two hearings of a number of extracts. The brevity of both extracts and questions in a thirty-minute paper means that superficiality is inevitable and that there will be a resultant lowering of standards. Only the LEAG syllabus caters for the more able, with one printed extract and four questions arising, and with two other general questions for which prior preparation is definitely needed and longer answers required. However, with these to justify a maximum of 10% of the examination, one wonders how many candidates will think the effort worthwhile.

There is a philosophy underlying this approach which is musically erroneous but unfortunately typical: that the detailed knowledge of a piece of music is merely another form of listening, if a more acute one. So the questions can justifiably be based on heard extracts. This is to downgrade the value, even necessity, of looking at the written score. It is akin to thinking that a play can be understood only if seen in a live performance. Obviously, music is written to be performed and heard, but some of the finest music stands a more detailed observation of the score, if only because the human mind cannot absorb at one hearing everything that takes place in, for example, a movement from a symphony, but focuses on individual parts or sections. The danger of the approach in the GCSE is that the candidate is questioned on what is heard at the time and not on his knowledge of how the music is composed, although a few questions, by way of compensation, on the techniques of the score are asked.

Elsewhere, one looks almost in vain for any question which requires anything resembling an essay. The Northern Examining Association syllabus provides the nearest to it, but unfortunately does not offer the option of the set work(s). The most there is to find in the MEG Syllabus 'B' is a 'free-response question which requires a response extending beyond one sentence'! In the SEG syllabus too, most tests require one-word answers or occasionally answers for which a few lines are provided. The questions on Musical Perception in the LEAG Syllabus, on its own admission, 'test candidate's understanding of music at an elementary level'. A section entitled Musical Literacy is more searching, involving aural recognition for which musical understanding is asked rather than a vague, general description. (A previously unheard piece is played ten times with ten questions arising from it.) The SEG gives a weighty equivalent to these two sections of 32% which is more than the 30% given each to Performing and Listening (the remaining 8% go on the two set works). This seems excessively high considering the nature of the questions.

It is an emotional or aesthetic response that is at the heart of what is looked for, as the SEC guide explicitly says:

> It would be the conviction of the candidate demonstrated in a response accurately related ... and well communicated that would gain credit, whether expressed in technical language or not.[5]

This is the justification therefore for the kind of non-descript question one finds in the NEA specimen paper: 'What do you like or dislike about this piece of music?' A number of questions are couched in factual terms, albeit simplistic ones. However, factual knowledge is made subservient to the aesthetic response, something which is widely open to abuse in youth if the mind is not trained to discern and balance on a basis of fact. Two questions in MEG specimen paper 'A' exemplify this: 'Music C sounds lively and happy because ...' and, in connection with soundtracks for three photographic scenes, 'The music is most suited to the soundtrack for Scene ... because ....' The SEC guide contains the following statements: 'The pupil's judgements must be accepted and valued'[6] and 'Auditory awareness and discrimination are at their best in youth.'[7] Logic and human experience deny the truth of the second statement. Auditory awareness has to be trained and discrimination developed as the child is exposed to music, whilst being given bases on which to do so. If the second statement were true, what is the role of the music teacher? As further evidence of the lesser importance which the GCSE attaches to the acquisition of musical knowledge as an end in itself, one may cite the kinds of infantile answer required by a question such as 'which of the following shapes looks like the melody?' (This is followed by a selection of arrows and jagged lines from which the candidate chooses that which most resembles the melody.) Or again: 'Indicate the pitch directions between the first five notes of this extract.' (The candidate is instructed to chart in a vague manner the direction of the pitch.) Such nebulous questions are the direct consequence of an unqualified belief in the truth of the first statement.

Presenting such a wide variety of music to such a wide range of ability makes it impossible to cater adequately for everybody. The difficulties in asking the 'right' questions will mean that the most able will have to answer questions which they will find ludicrously simple, and other candidates will have been trained by teachers to avoid those they cannot do. The true aural abilities of all candidates will not have been fathomed.

Performing

Few would argue that the inclusion of practical skills in a public music examination is a bad thing. The GCE and CSE syllabuses have recognised it for some time. In the O-Level for example, up to 25% may be accounted for by passing an

external examination such as that set by the Associated
Board of the Royal Schools of Music. GCSE raises this
percentage, which seems attractive enough. However, the
approach is very different. In keeping with its general
philosophy, it is the process of performing that is of essence
rather than the product of a performance. So internal
assessment for most syllabuses is encouraged over a period
of time. Theoretically, a candidate may perform on
whatever instrument any number of times during that
period, the best performance of which may count towards
the final examination result. A teacher may, similarly,
assess a performance bearing in mind the preparation
leading to it, and extraneous factors. However reasonable
and encouraging all this sounds, it is musically untenable.
Musicians are inevitably judged on single performances,
however difficult they may have found the practice and
despite not feeling well on the day. It is the performance
that is to be judged, not the performer or the process of
performing. We are doing future musicians a disservice if
we cushion them from the disciplines and realities of
performing.

There is a further difference in that GCSE seeks to give
recognition to corporate music making by giving marks for
singing/playing in an ensemble and rehearsing/directing an
ensemble. It also gives recognition to improvisation as live
composition. All three, together with the more traditional
tests of solo performance, sight-reading and ear tests, are
options from which the candidate chooses a certain number.
These traditional tests are given a weighting of only 18%,
the solo performance often being limited to one piece, in
which it is more difficult to assess a candidate's performing
ability than in the three pieces and scales required by the
Associated Board.

Assessment

When one considers the question of assessment in Performing and Composing, problems of guaranteeing, and agreeing upon, a fair, representative grade for candidates become evident. To begin with, musicianship is somehow separated from, and elevated above, technical accomplishment. This is surely erroneous; the two are intimately linked, the one being a vehicle for the other. The National Criteria tell us that 'it must be possible for candidates who have received no instrumental tuition outside the GCSE course to achieve high grades in the examination.' Given that those who receive such tuition outside the classroom are at an advantage, the SEC Guide chooses to advocate that this objective is fulfilled by an assessment of 'musical sensitivity and experience'. The assessment of performance is difficult enough anyway being so much a matter of personal response, but it is no answer to pretend that the advantage does not or should not exist. The SEC Guide actually devalues technical achievement and, I contend, will lower standards by this and by the following remarks: 'The Examining Groups will ensure that the criteria they use for judging the performing skills of candidates are not set with unrealistic standards in mind.'[8] The Guide differentiates between the assessment of the musical and the technical by stating later: 'Any assessment of music should be about what is intrinsically musical – that which gives it the power of expression' (which surely includes technique, be it instrumental or compositional). The Guide then claims that: 'Many aspects of past or current examinations in music have not conformed to this basic expectation' – an accusation which is questionable.

By such differentiation, the Guide strikes deeply at the

heart of what it is to be a true musician. The true musician is motivated by reaching for the ideal of his art. Everything he does or hears is in comparison with an ideal, and failure to reach it is recognised as such and then used as a stepping stone to improve his art. If musical standards are to mean anything, listener, performer and composer alike judge many skills, both technical and interpretive. Where there is progress towards that ideal, appreciation and credit are given. One cannot judge only 'on the positive qualities of the performance rather than on failure to reach some hypothetic ideal'.[10] Both are sides of the same coin.

How is one to assess one person's performance in an ensemble? That depends on the constitution of that ensemble, the nature of the music and on the various contributions of the members of that ensemble. And how is assessment to be made of rehearsal and direction? That depends for one thing on whether it is a first or final rehearsal and on the choice of music. Now, music making has a social aspect, but whether this aspect should be examined is questionable. A teacher's written report or guarantee concerning a candidate's corporate musical acti-vities would suffice. I am not trying to provide answers to these and other questions, but merely to point out the inconsistencies that have inevitably arisen when one is testing an individual contribution in and to a group performance, be it as performer or director.

There are three particular examples on the tape which accompanies the SEC Guide which illustrate the problems. Two are to be assessed as solo performances, yet are part of ensembles. To me, there is no difference between these and a third example which contains a performance to be assessed as part of an ensemble. Nor should there be different criteria for this third example, because a perform-ance is to be judged on its own merits, including both the

individual contribution and that contribution to the ensemble. All three are in a popular idiom, as the others on the
tape are also. The first two performances are praised and,
we are told, could expect to be given high grades. When a
group of about thirty teachers practised assessing these
songs, there was a wide discrepancy between the marks
given. Clearly, not all agreed with the SEC Guide, and
understandably: the first performer sings only two different
phrases in the course of the song, the first of which is two
bars, and the second, four bars. Her total contribution to
the song is only sixteen bars. The second performer sings
something more substantial, but the musical style of both
songs severely limits and handicaps the performers. Yet the
grades are made comparable with a grade five pass in an
Associated Board Examination. I do not propose to criticise
the individual performances but merely point out the
lowering of standards.

In the assessment of rehearsal and direction, two Examining Groups interpret the Criteria completely different-
ly. MEG states that assessment will be made on one
rehearsal and then performance, any previous rehearsals
being acknowledged. SEG gives specific instructions that
the music must have been previously unrehearsed as an
ensemble, although it may be seen by the individual
participants one week beforehand. The assessment is then
of the first rehearsal. The two groups differ again on
whether the choice of music should affect the assessment.
The Southern Group says that 'the difficulty of the piece is
not in itself an aspect of the assessment but will affect the
task.' The Midland says unequivocally 'that the difficulty of
the individual parts ... must be taken into account' and to
that end introduces a 'difficulty multiplier' (as it does for
Prepared Performance). Of course, the difficulty and
quality of the music is bound to affect the assessment! How

can one compare the directing of a large ensemble playing fast music with complex rhythms, for example (where the function of the conductor may be just to keep the time), and the directing of a hymn-tune arranged for a string quartet (where the rehearsal may be more concerned with balance, tuning and phrasing)? The music for the one is more difficult than the other, but the direction is the other way round. Only the LEAG and Welsh syllabuses save the teacher from facing these issues in Performing by providing an external examiner. This does not, however, seem quite within the spirit of the examination.

When one couples these kinds of inconsistencies with the wide diversity available in both instrumental and compositional styles, and the problems of comparison inherent in this diversity, musical standards are likely to be blurred. The assessor is being asked to 'identify those attributes of performing which are common to all types and styles and which may therefore form the basis of any assessment of performance, prepared or unprepared.'[11] The same could be said of the assessment of Composition. This generalist approach is just not possible in practice because different styles demand different methods and techniques. The assessor is given compartments in order to make the assessment as objective as possible, yet is supposed, in composition at least, to go beyond that to the 'more important assessment of the power of the music to move emotions – to engage people in musical experience'.[12] A suggested list of the attributes of performing in all styles includes 'clarity of intention' and 'sense of conviction and involvement'.[13] What *do* all these things mean? And why are musicianship, phrasing, and melodic shape not mentioned? A tribal war-song, a child singing a nursery rhyme and a rendering of Auld Lang Syne in a public house all fulfil these guidelines admirably. Furthermore, GCSE makes them the legitimate products of classroom activity and could allow such products about two thirds of the examination, and therefore of the course.

Composing

The importance attached to Composition is the most obviously novel feature of the new examination. GCE invited submissions of candidates' own work, and composing has been present in the CSE syllabuses. However, in GCSE there are some clear differences.

Part of the A-Level and degree courses in music has traditionally been the study of Harmony and Counterpoint to effect a mastery of past musical styles and forms. Composers of the past have learned their art too by acquaintance with and mastery of such styles. Bach, for example, copied out the orchestral works of Vivaldi. This century, one has only to think of Britten and Berkeley, both of whom had lessons from other composers and wrote pastiche. They then showed in their own compositions that they had understood those styles and were able to use them for their own ends. This disciplined learning was just as important in the creation of their best music as their own immediate inspiration. Few composers have been completely self-taught. One looks in vain for such a learning process in the GCSE. The study of any traditional harmony and form is no longer required. Even the use of staff notation is no longer compulsory, although candidates must be familiar with it to a modest degree in their 'listening'. 'Other forms of notation should not be excluded', state the National Criteria, and used if appropriate. This guarantees little and gives a let-out to those who would choose not to teach it or recommend its use, and to those who would rather not submit to the discipline. In practice, some of our higher-graded candidates in GCSE may not be able to use, or may not have been trained in some of the mechanics of our art, preferring instead to use something more immediate, a graphic notation perhaps, but something less universal and certainly something less tried and tested.

What replaces these composition techniques? Anything, it seems. 'All genres and traditions are to be encouraged.' Beginning with the experience of the child, or from any very simple starting point, the learning is by discovery and self-criticism. The teacher's role is now to guide the formulation of the composer's intentions, not to teach. Group work is encouraged, as are the performances of compositions to others in the class. Traditional academic procedures are therefore not referred to, except where relevant. There is some value in this approach to a point, but where it assumes the properties that it does in the GCSE, and given the drawbacks in the remainder of the examination criteria, there is a great imbalance. The end result will be children who are not schooled in musical technique and who will simply create music that they find appealing and in tune with their own experience.

The definition of composition provided by the same music advisor referred to earlier and which epitomised the concept of composition to which this new examination gives official credence does not go far enough. Composition, he said, is 'the exploration of sound used for expression purposes'. The definition provided by the National Criteria that composition is 'the creation and organisation of sound based on stimuli chosen by the pupil or by the teacher' is only marginally better. Children will naturally veer towards writing music with which they may have a more immediate initial affinity, towards idioms which rely heavily on an improvisational style and on more simple forms, tonal and harmonic structures. They will veer away likewise from building up larger works from small musical ideas, and from the more disciplined and demanding approach required by more complex harmonic styles. We should remember, however, that not all that is unappealing and difficult is without reward.

GCSE seems to be more concerned to reflect the popular cultures of today, by bringing them into the classroom, than it is to educate. I have heard, on two separate training days for teachers, examples of such compositions which have disturbed me and which are examples of this unsound educational philosophy. Both were rock songs, where words and music were composed by the pupils. The first was heavily occultic in its inspiration (the words are printed in the SEC Guide). The words of the second (brought by a colleague on a tape recording), I found repulsive – akin to material one might find in a horror film. GCSE validates both as the results of legitimate classroom activity, and proclaims them as educationally valuable. It is tripping up over itself in order to avoid judging music which may actually be less than beneficial to children. When there is so much good music which is worth studying, why does the new examination seek to justify what is, in comparison, rubbish?

The inclusion of Improvisation in the examination also raises its problems. It is included under Performing, but it is essentially creative. Is the teacher to judge the creativity or the performance? And, if the former, which I suggest it should be, to what extent can the limitation of the candidate's technical ability affect an assessment? Improvisation seeks to justify the value of a first attempt, live, to compose. I do not question here the musical value of those styles in music, such as jazz, in which improvisation plays such a large role. But I do question the worth of including this practice on one instrument in the context of an examination. First live attempts at composition are seldom the best, and I fear that its inclusion is another attempt by those who have formulated the Criteria to let anything pass as worthy of classroom activity.

Conclusion

The new examination has its followers, undoubtedly. However, considerable unease and opposition to it exist amongst a number of musicians with whom I have talked. Teachers, too, have grave misgivings, judging by the reactions of many I have heard on the various phases of the training in preparation for it. Fortunately, the Criteria and syllabuses are on the whole sufficiently broad to allow teachers to teach and to maintain the standards in which they believe. Our children *need* not suffer. However, in the wrong hands, there could be abuse, and it is the serious possibility of this which I am concerned to expose. With their desire to make music accessible to all, those who have drawn up the examination have over-emphasised musical activity and experience to the detraction of everything else. They have not ensured a balance, at least, in what is taught. This is not exactly the freedom from bias which is called for by the General Criteria! Certainly, the examination is not really appropriate for the most able musician, which it purports to be. I fear that a number of others too in this new generation of examinees could end up musically ill-disciplined and ill-equipped, having only an insubstantial knowledge of the mechanics of music and, perhaps most important of all, without the capacity to appreciate, respect and understand our rich cultural heritage.

PART TWO

PART TWO

6. THE GCSE PHILOSOPHY OF EDUCATION[1.]

Anthony O'Hear

I was writing this piece on the very day that the Secretary of State for Education announced the introduction of a core curriculum in schools, with tests for pupils at the ages of 7, 11 and 14. Once the scheme is implemented, it appears that a child will be able to move from a school in one part of the country to one in another and pick up just where he left off. I was interested to notice that the core curriculum does not seem to extend beyond the age of 14, presumably because any such thing would be difficult to integrate with the GCSE. For most subjects the GCSE National Criteria do not lay down any detailed curriculum content. Rather, they stress 'aims' and 'assessment objectives', and the generally rather indeterminate content instructions are, in the words of the Science Criteria, little more than a general exhortation that 'any syllabus (should) provide an appropriate vehicle of the Aims and Assessment Objectives'. The History Criteria are quite explicit in stating that it is 'not desirable to stipulate a minimum core of content' in order to allow 'freedom to innovate' and to 'reflect local interests'. There would not be much chance there for a child to slip easily from a school in Haringey to one in Harrogate, any more than there would be in Classical Subjects, where not even a general overview of the history of Greece and Rome is stipulated, or in Religious Studies where syllabuses are to be based on 'the study of one, two or three of the major world religions' (which, for this purpose, include Sikhism, but not Confucianism, Taoism or Jainism).

I imagine that many people who have heard of the GCSE only in general terms would be surprised at all this talk of syllabuses in the plural. Is not the GCSE being promoted as one universal examination, for all pupils? But appearances are delusory. There may be one examination, but in one examination there are many modes of assessment, many syllabuses and many levels of aspiration and achievement. Indeed, under the third of the three modes of assessment (Mode 3 examinations), any school is allowed to submit its own syllabus for any given subject, while different papers and questions of differing difficulty within a given examination will be given to candidates of differing ability. Even under Mode 1 assessment, where papers are set by an examining authority, a 'significant' percentage of the marks will be given for coursework set and assessed internally by teachers in the schools of candidates. Moreover, considerable emphasis is placed on project work, often on themes selected by pupils themselves and on topics of local interest. Thus, for example, the SEC teachers' guide to Geography suggests a school litter survey, History the study of a local church, English the study of a local newspaper, and so on. Further, candidates of lower ability will, in some subjects, be allowed to take papers which will entitle them only to one of the lower grades. While many people would find this arrangement eminently sensible, it does, of course, go against the egalitarian ideology which informs the publicity for the GCSE, if not its actual rationale, as a single examination accessible to 'the great majority of the general school population'. For why, apart from egalitarian prejudice, would one expect such a thing to be a possible or desirable goal after 11 years of compulsory education? The GCSE is, in fact, the logical outcome of comprehensivisation, but like the comprehensive system itself, conceals a multiplicity of difference of standards, of abilities and of attainment and aspiration behind a single façade. With the GCSE, one does not as yet know whether the uniformity of outer shell will lead to an interior levelling down of the best, as many believe to have been the case in the comprehensive system, without any sign of a compensatory levelling up of the worst; or whether the multiplicity of actual differences within each examination concealed behind the bland outer clothing of a 'GCSE certificate' will lead to a completely anarchic situation, in which genuine comparisons between pupils become virtually impossible – for the public at least; or whether, perhaps, in the worst of all worlds, both these unfortunate things will happen, which would, of course, be one way of bringing about the desired egalitarian outcome.

I may be accused of unfairness in so questioning the results of the introduction of the GCSE almost before it has even started. In truth, I do not know whether it will have the results just envisaged. Nor am I convinced that a national core curriculum is so very desirable, as opposed to other less draconian ways of achieving the same goal of high and reliable standards in education, such as a national examination system designed to test a significant breadth and depth of knowledge and understanding in the areas examined. My main reservation about the GCSE is that in the National Criteria and in the supplementary literature put out by the Second Examinations Council (SEC) (which is the body overseeing the GCSE) there is a more or less wholesale abandonment of the idea of education as an initiation into existing forms of worthwhile knowledge and understanding. Instead, stress is laid on the pursuit of goals of 'relevance' and of the acquisition of the so-called 'skills' of judgement, evaluation of data, and personal enquiry and assessment. Such 'skills' are bound to be empty and

ill-informed if not based in any real immersion in existing
forms of knowledge. The general aims of most subject
criteria are framed in terms of a Deweyesque educational
philosophy, in which understanding and knowledge of a
subject (dismissively referred to as mere 'recall' or 'passive
learning') is regarded as inert and useless unless it stems
from and can be related to some real-life problem or activity
which a beginner has or can engage in. We are told in the
SEC *Guide to the GCSE* that there was a need to change
from traditional forms of examining and teaching which
called for learning facts at the expense of understanding, as
if there could be any effective understanding of an area of
knowledge that did not involve a firm factual basis. But not
according to the GCSE. Thus, in the Geography Criteria,
for example, 'recall' is to count for only 20%-40% of the
marks given, while 'skills' (of 'selecting techniques relevant
to a geographical enquiry') are to count for 20%-40%, as
are 'practical skills' (however assessed). In History, too,
great stress is laid on 'essential study skills, such as the
ability to locate and extract information from primary and
secondary sources; to detect bias; to analyse this information and construct a logical argument ('usually through the
medium of writing') – as if these 'study skills' could be
detached from 'the acquisition of knowledge and understanding', and as if 'recall' of such knowledge was not a *sine
qua non* for effectively detecting bias and the rest in any
document or bit of evidence one was presented with. That is
to say, even an experienced historian would hardly be able
to do any of that with assurance when faced with evidence
from a period about which he knew nothing, while his
assurance that a source was biased would increase with the
amount of countervailing evidence he had to hand. Indeed,
it might be well to press this point, and to insist, with
Wittgenstein in *On Certainty*, that the testing and confirm-

ing of evidence and hypothesis always takes place within a system of *knowledge*. Before the child has grasped quite a lot of the system, its questioning of evidence is merely otiose and holds up its progress. There is indeed a danger that the GCSE's stress on the exercise of judgement by what are, after all, beginners in their subjects will actually impede the acquisition of that mature exercise of judgement which comes from a firm grounding in one's subject, producing instead the modish and ignorant scepticism of the journalist or first year undergraduate. It is in any case scarcely to be envisaged that the average 16 year old will be able to 'recognise the usefulness and limitations of the scientific method' and that 'the study and practice of science are subject to various limitations and uncertainties' (as the aims of the National Criteria for Science would have it), when not even the core content of the Physics Criteria contains any reference to either the theory of Relativity or to Quantum Theory.

As we will see in more detail later, the GCSE aims and objectives are largely based on the assumption that there can be effective learning only when what is learned either stems from some problem arising from the experience of the learner, or can be seen as relevant to something in the learner's personal or social world. Thus, we are instructed in section 19(k) of the General Criteria for *all* GCSE examinations (entitled 'Emphases to be encouraged in all subjects') that:

> all syllabuses should be designed to help candidates to understand the subject's relationship to other areas of study and its relevance to the candidate's own life.

Both the holism and the narrowness of this instruction are to be observed. As would no doubt be expected, the relationship to other areas of study is glossed in the next sentence as 'awareness of economic, political, social and environmental factors' relevant to the subject concerned, while any hope that formal education might be a process by which the candidate can for a time forget his own life and its petty relevances in order to enter wider and more inclusive imaginative worlds is presumably to be dashed by a neurotic and teacher-led absorption in one's own life and its problems (or supposed problems). Worst of all is the underlying assumption that something is worth learning only if it can be related to one's own life. Any vision of a form of knowledge or of culture as worthwhile just in so far as it can be detached from 'economic, political, social and environmental factors' and worth learning just because it has no immediate relevance to one's own life is precluded by the dogmatism of paragraph 19(k).

Yet such a vision is both eminently defensible and lies at the very heart of what has traditionally been thought of as liberal education. Take, for example, the study of physics, or indeed of any part of the natural sciences. The aim of such study is the discovery of the nature of the natural world, and while it is true that natural scientists are human beings in specific economic, political, social and environmental circumstances, circumstances which may have affected the way they worked and theorised, the value and significance of their work and theories, *qua* natural science, is quite independent of those factors. And, of course, in the West, since the time of Galileo, a mature theoretical physics has developed, with its own momentum and problems, which transcend the social and political backgrounds of the scientists involved: such things impinge only as irritants to or diversions from the main task: the theoretical understanding of natural processes. Nor are we to suppose that Newton or Einstein or Bohr asked themselves how relevant their studies were to their own lives, or that if they had asked themselves this question, it would have had any bearing on their or other scientists' assessment of the truth or falsity of their theories. The point I am making here is simply the familiar one, that if one wants to understand the achievements of a mature science, one must learn to understand the theories and confirmation procedures of that science, and the same goes for mathematics.

No doubt there are questions which could be asked about the external history of a science (the history, that is to say, of the social and personal background of scientists) and also about its technological effects and the social consequences of technology. But these questions are quite separate from the theoretical understanding of nature delivered by a science, and anyone who wants to understand that must prescind from these other questions. The GCSE science syllabuses unfortunately regularly conflate the two types of question in their efforts to obey instruction 19(k). In the SEC's own guide for teachers on GCSE Science, for example, an approach to Chemistry is commended which is based on 'issues that students find important in their own and others lives'; predictably the list includes: nuclear energy; lead in petrol; acid rain; destruction of the ozone layer; food and fertilisers (including the 'world food problem' and 'butter mountains'); cosmetics ('rabbits don't cry'); drugs; and, finally, 'Whatever happened to British Steel?' I shall leave it to others to comment on the politically loaded nature of this list (and also of the Haringey Multicultural Biology Group's diagram, repro-duced on page 9 of the Science brochure, and of questions like that in a specimen Art paper telling pupils to design a mural for a village involved in the miners' strike). But it is clear that any sense that the primary aim of scientific activity and its study is the structured understanding of an aspect of nature which can be produced by disinterested enquiry has here been abandoned. Of course, once one loses the sense that some sort of disinterested knowledge of the structure of nature has been achieved through scientific enquiry then political bias and sociological analysis can rule the roost unchecked; but to lose this sense is to lose just what is distinctive and worthwhile about science and its study, and to fail in what should be the primary aim and justification of science education.

I am not actually clear from the Aims section of the National Criteria for Science syllabuses (which all the particular sciences are governed by) whether initiation into the *theoretical* understanding of nature is recognised as being an aim of GCSE science at all. These aims specify study of 'experimental and practical science' to enable pupils to become 'confident citizens in a technological world', to recognise the usefulness and limitations of science (as we have seen), to develop skills and abilities that are 'relevant to the study of science', 'to stimulate curiosity, interest and enjoyment in science' and its methods, 'interest in and care for the environment' and an awareness of the social and historical influences and 'limitations' of science, and of the benefits and harms caused by the technological applications of science. The study of experimental and practical science envisaged would appear to place a very large emphasis on those types of experiments and observations which pupils could devise and execute for themselves, and it is far from clear that the sort of low-level, largely factual and analytic investigation one would expect here, into the type of topic mentioned in the SEC guide such as the rusting of bridges, the running of milk floats, and the strength and absorbency of types of paper, has anything at all in common with the sort of imagination-led theorising and speculation that has characterised the major scientific achievements of men such as Galileo, Kepler, Newton,

Darwin, Einstein and the rest, which have led to our present understanding of nature. Whether they have or not, it is pretty clear that GCSE students are not going to be allowed near them, except in so far as they fall under the rubric of 'stimulating curiosity' (or provide fodder for the socio-historical researches of multicultural biology and the like). If one wanted evidence of a recent decline in educational standards and aspirations, one need look no further than the GCSE's characterisation of the educational aim of entering the imaginative understanding of nature vouchsafed to us by the work of Galileo and his successors over the last 400 years, as a matter of stimulating 'curiosity, interest and enjoyment in science and its methods of study'.

One might have thought that mathematics was an area in which learning at the age of 15 could be safely structured in terms of the concepts and proofs arrived at in mathematical study. Here at least, results are nothing if not well-founded, and understanding of the results derivable most securely from a firm grasp of the mathematically canonical methods of proof and construction. While the National Criteria for mathematics, which include an unusually long and detailed core content, might lead one to hope that here at least formal, structured initiation would be the teaching and examining norm, the SEC *Guide to the GCSE* officiously informs us that:

> traditionally, mathematics has been about knowing the rules to deal with numbers, percentages, areas, equations, and so on. It has often been divided into arithmetic, algebra and geometry. GCSE should lead pupils to see that mathematics can be used to solve practical problems in everyday situations.... One approach is to let pupils explore their own ways of using what they know about numbers, shapes, and so on, rather than insisting that results are reached by one fixed, ideal method.

Where notions of proof and truth are as clear and well-defined as they are in mathematics, one wonders just what is envisaged by this disparagement of 'fixed, ideal' methods, referred to elsewhere in the SEC guide as 'didactic' teaching, as if teachers were wrong to be didactic. Are invalid ways of reaching results as good for the purposes of the GCSE as valid ones? Are empirical generalisations just as good as formal proofs? And while no one would ever have denied that mathematics has practical applications in the real world, it is surely important to indicate, even to 15 and 16 year olds, the ways in which mathematical work is not constrained by its empirical applications, but in many ways mysteriously transcends the empirical world altogether. Indeed, in mathematics (as in natural science) one often cannot know or foresee just which researches will turn out to have empirical applications. Modern computing is based on the pre-war work of Turing and Church into what were at the time regarded as the utterly arcane topics of decidability and the discovery of very large prime numbers. (Needless to say, GCSE Computing Studies makes no mention whatever of the theoretical basis of computing.) The SEC's view of mathematics has been worth considering because it is symptomatic of the GCSE approach generally, with its preference for discovery methods and exploration at the expense of formal teaching. Now, discovery methods have their home, if anywhere, in the primary stages of education. They are clearly inappropriate if one intends serious initiation into well-established bodies of knowledge. At best they are time-consuming and wasteful of effort; at worst they are designed to ensure that pupils will actually discover very little of what is known and has been discovered over long periods of time. It is hardly to be expected that even the most intelligent 16 year old will discover for himself Pythagoras's theorem, or

Newton's laws or the theory of Relativity, or even how to fire a pot. And why, merest prejudice aside, is it thought desirable that he should? Serious matters and serious traditions demand serious apprenticeships, not the play of the primary school. At senior secondary school level such approaches will simply conspire to cut pupils off from the cultural achievements of mankind, and all because of the block-headed insistence of Dewey and his followers that all genuine education experiences must stem from the real-life experiences of the learner.

Unless 'experience' is taken in an utterly vacuous sense, to cover anything a learner might absorb, the insistence that interest in a subject can be stimulated only from within one's 'real life' experience is itself simply untrue to experience, as the current crazes for space sagas and high-life soap operas testifies. And why should educators aim lower than the mass media in their efforts to expand the mind of pupils? And what more genuinely educative experience could one envisage than the following:

> The lecturer was talking about matters and things in the world of art, situations that had never come within our horizon and only appeared now on its margin in shadowy wise through the always compromised medium of his speech. We were unable to check up on it except through his own explanatory performances on the cottage piano, and we listened to it all with dimly excited fantasy of children hearing a fairy story they do not understand, while their tender minds are none the less in a strange, dreamy, intuitive way enriched and advantaged. Fugue, counterpoint, 'Eroica', 'confusion in consequence of too strongly coloured modulations', 'strict style' – all that was just magic spells to us, but we heard it as greedily, as large-eyed, as children always hear what they do not understand or what is even entirely unsuitable – indeed with far more pleasure than the familiar, fitting and adequate can given them. Is it believable that this is the most intensive, splendid, perhaps

the most productive way of learning: the anticipatory way, learning that spans wide stretches of ignorance? As a pedagogue, I suppose I should not speak in its behalf....

The pedagogue here is Dr Serenus Zeitblom, Thomas Mann's pedantic narrator in his *Doctor Faustus*, and he is talking about the lectures on Beethoven given by the town organist Wendel Kretschmar that he and his friend, the future composer Adrian Leverkuhn, went to as young boys. Scrupulous pedagogues need have no Zeitblom-like fears, though, when it comes to GCSE Music, that pupils will be exposed to the dangerous anticipatory way of learning, for the National Criteria for Music insist that Music syllabuses must 'admit those areas of musical experience in which pupils admit keen interest', so pop music is to be admitted to the syllabus if this is where pupils have keen interest. This type of playing down to the lowest level is typical of the GCSE – the English Literature criteria allow for 'wide personal choice' in set text, and insist that set texts need be no longer prescribed. In practical areas of the syllabus, candidates are to be allowed to perform music of their own choice and to compose in any style they 'may wish to offer', submitting 'annotated tapes' if they do not feel like scoring their compositions, or learning how to score them.

It is possible that some Music teachers will continue to base their work on what the SEC teaching guide on Music ignorantly refers to as the 'classical Western-European tradition of Music', (Tchaikovsky, Mussorgsky, Chopin, Mahler, Smetana, Janacek, Bartok and Sibelius all being Western Europeans, presumably, in the collective mind of the SEC, whereas actually they were the artists they were just because they were *not* Western Europeans). Such teachers may feel that this tradition is incomparably rich and expressive, one of the unquestioned triumphs of the human spirit, and one peculiarly rooted in that post-

Renaissance civilisation to which we are privileged to be heirs; and, further, that they have a duty to concentrate in their teaching on initiating young people into the riches of this tradition. I wish such teachers well, because they would certainly be admonished by the writers of the SEC guide to GCSE Music not merely for failing to recognise the alleged 'cultural diversity' of modern Britain, but also for failing to prepare for their students the 'much better balance in the musical diet' which the National Criteria for Music require. In the new GCSE world, then, Bach will be balanced by Wham and Bob Marley, Verdi by Mantovani and Frank Sinatra, Wagner by a bit of Afro-Rock and Chopin by the odd classical Indian raga. The authors of the teachers' guide admit that this abandoning of traditional music education 'may take us into unknown territory'; this I regard not as commendable modesty, but as an entirely frivolous attitude on the part of those intent on denying young people a serious opportunity to enter one of the most precious achievements of our civilisation.

I have argued that the socio-historical approach and the quest for relevance is inappropriate in a study of the natural sciences, largely on the grounds that the mature and disinterested study of the natural world, which has flourished since the sixteenth century, must be understood on its own terms first, if it is to be understood at all. A sociologist or historian might watch the activities of scientists for as long as he likes; but unless he grasps the scientific problems the scientists are wrestling with and the scientific theories they are developing and testing he will fail to grasp the point of their activity and the nature of their judgements, in much the same way as one would fail to grasp the nature of a game like football if one simply looked at the private lives, mutual interaction and social mobility of footballers. Socio-historical considerations might have a bearing on the technological applications of science, but to treat them as the main focus of a study of science is to collude in the popular misconception that one can change the natural world without understanding its nature, that applied science can somehow be produced without a firm theoretical basis. It is also to fail to recognise the educational and human values involved in learning to pursue the truth about the world without ulterior motive; something for which, for all its blemishes and distortions, natural science still stands as a symbol and inspiration.

It might, though, be felt that when we come to consider the human world, as represented by the studies of history, literature, the arts, religion and the social sciences, there is something far more plausible about considering what we study in terms of its social roots and in terms of its relevance to our students. After all, are not the works of man rooted in his history and society, and is not their worth to us constituted by the ways they are relevant to our own lives?

As to the first point, there can be no denying that human works have social and historical roots, and in many cases to understand those roots will be to understand more about the work. But it is far from clear that understanding those roots is always equivalent to understanding what is important about a work of art or literature. The National Criteria for Art and Design tell us that one of the aims of Art education is to develop 'awareness and appreciation of the relationships between Art and the individual within the historical, social and environmental context': there is little hint here that the nature of the relationship between some artists and their context might be one of transcendence of context. There were a thousand talented painters of domestic scenes in seventeenth century Holland, but only one Vermeer, and Vermeer speaks to us as more than a mere representative of his time. There is in Vermeer something more than mere relevance to his context. And the same goes for some works of literature. *King Lear* is certainly not about the early history of England, but neither is it about problems and situations peculiar to the early seventeenth century. What it deals with and discloses is far more universal and far less context-dependent than that, and was for that very reason set by Shakespeare in a mythical time. One's worry about the constant exhortations in the GCSE criteria and guides to stimulate awareness of context is that it is going to lead to studies of art and literature which prevent the student from seeing oil paintings, say, as anything other than a symptom of the obsession of a rising bourgeoisie to possess and display. Such an attitude not only overlooks the way a work of art can transcend its time or be implicitly or explicitly critical of its historical context; it also signally fails to recognise the way in which in art, just as in science, a style and a tradition can generate its own standards, problems and expressive power in a way autonomous of historical context. The growth of harmonic music might or might not have had something to do with the development of capitalist society, but such generalising banalities can tell us nothing about the poignancy of a modulation in a Chopin nocturne. The eighteenth century country house is as much a product of its time and class as the contemporary office block, but one would expect a course on Art and Design to concentrate on explaining the respects in which the one is beautiful and the other brutal, rather than on the historical circumstances of their modes of production. The GCSE criteria do not explicitly rule out the cultivation of aesthetic taste and judgement, but one fears this may well be the effect of the dreary insistence on examining the sociological background to art and literature (as in every other area of study), as well as of the talk in the SEC guide of the potential of Art and

Design courses to contribute to the development of anti-racist and anti-sexist policies and to indicate 'ways in which images of women reinforce sexual stereotyping'. It is clear that against this sort of background, the chances of studying works of art and literature as assessable on their own terms, and as valuable (or not) for what they are in themselves is very low; and thus the potential widening of experience afforded us by the disinterested study of works of art and entry into their imaginative worlds for their own sake will be denied to GCSE pupils.

Even if under the GCSE, the study of art and literature will not inevitably become sociologised, they will inevitably be contaminated by the search for the relevance of any work study to one's own life. Section 19 (k) of the General Criteria is, as we have seen, insistent that the study of art and literature is, like all else, to be made relevant to the candidate's own life. Equally, in History, study of the past is to be linked with the present, in Classical Studies we are to acquire an awareness of the differences and similarities between 'the classical civilisation studied and one's own', while in Religious Studies, candidates are expected to 'express an opinion of their own' on 'matters of religious belief and practice' though without the validity of their viewpoint being assessed. (All these requirements are in the National Criteria for the respective subjects.) I do not deny that anything one studies of the human world of history, art and religion has, in a broad sense, relevance to one's own life. But this sense can be very broad indeed, and only to be impeded by a constant and intrusive looking back at oneself when one's gaze should be directed at works and deeds which are worth studying precisely because they have no obvious or direct connection with one's own life. One of the virtues of our studying the civilisation of classical Greece is that in doing so we can look at a civilisation which, while not utterly foreign to our civilisation, being in some ways an ancestor of our own, is both dead (and hence a highly suitable object of disinterested study) and in many ways greater than our own. We are judged by it, and we grasp it just in so far as we submit to its discipline and its meanings and values. The mind-broadening effect of coming into contact with the stones and texts of ancient Greece would be vitiated if we were forever busily expressing opinions about it and relating it to our own lives. And the same goes for any genuine insight into a religion and its relation to a culture. This is something not to be achieved by the inquisitive visitations by pupils to synagogues, mosques and temples and cemeteries, or by the comparative viewing of videos on Eastern Orthodoxy and Black Pentecostalism recommended by the SEC teacher's guide to Religious Studies. Understanding the meaning of a religion, and what role it really plays in the lives of its adherents demands a far more serious and respectful attitude to it than this sort of attention to its surface forms would allow; it would require, at the very least, some disciplined effort to understand its central texts and its history, and perhaps even to come to *reasoned* judgement about its dogmatic basis, though any such judgement would fall foul of the underlying presumption of the SEC teacher's guide to Religious Studies, according to which 'issues of belief and value are matters of *opinion*'. It is, presumably, for this reason that students' opinions on these matters are not to be tested for their validity, an insidious form of relativism examined by David Cooper in his article in this book.

My objection to the search for relevance in the study of history, literature and religion is, in fact, very well put in the passage from Frank Whitehead quoted by Jonathan Worthen in his article in this book:

Increasingly literature has been 'used' ... as a launching pad
to get children talking or writing about their own experiences ... (which seems) to me to imply an erosion of belief in
the power of literature as such, in the value of exposing
oneself to the impact of a poem or story or novel for its own
sake. At its worst the approach seems to carry with it an
assumption that anything a pupil says or writes after reading
a work of literature must somehow be relevant to it.[2]

It is not that a work of literature might not be 'relevant' to
one's own life. It is rather that if one approaches it with a
view to establishing what relevance it has to our own lives,
one is likely to fail to read it, and to fail to understand what
it has to offer, and what it really has to teach us. And yet,
reading something – and learning to read something – for its
own sake, on its own merits, appears to be forbidden by the
GCSE demand that teachers design their syllabuses so as to
show the relevance of a subject of study to pupils' own lives,
and also by the constant stress we find in the National
Criteria and related documents on 'active' and 'resource-
based' learning, as opposed to 'passive' learning and
'didactic' teaching. For learning *really* to read a text or to
understand a theory or to grasp the significance of some
aspect of the past, requires that the learner is subject to the
discipline and authority and knowledge of a true teacher.

It may, of course, be that the disciplined study of science,
of literature and of history in any shape or form is beyond
many of our secondary school pupils, although I would be
reluctant to accept such a blanket exclusion of the less able
from academic study too easily. But if this is so, and
educational theorists of both left and right have argued that
it is then non-academic curricula and examinations are
required for the less able (rather than as I would urge,
academic courses and examinations of differing difficulty).
The GCSE, by contrast, is tailoring the provision for all to

the needs or supposed needs of the least able in the ways I have indicated – by relating everything to the life-experiences of pupils, by encouraging the introduction of simplistic and often politicised socio-historical analyses into all fields of study, and by emphasising tasks pupils can undertake on their own and out of their own interests (or supposed interests), a clear case of the tail wagging the dog; a case, indeed, of the diet of the secondary school being rendered bland and tasteless by the methods of the primary school.

This last point indicates the way in which dilution of the academic approach has been seeping upwards through our educational system, like some form of rising damp. And it cannot stop at GCSE. Pupils who have taken the GCSE will be ill-fitted for A-Level courses, a point noted and commented on by the Committee of Vice-Chancellors and Principals of Universities in October 1986, through their then Chairman, Professor Maurice Shock. Professor Shock expected A-Levels to disappear in a few years time, and spoke of the need for radical changes in university courses to accommodate the new type of student, and to bring university courses into line with the GCSE approach to education. At least Professor Shock's intervention has the virtue of recognising what many still refuse to admit: that the GCSE does involve a radical change in educational methods and standards in secondary schools. As I have tried to indicate in this paper, despite disclaimers that are sometimes made, the Criteria for the GCSE will, if adhered to, make it impossible for teachers to adhere firmly and centrally to disciplined, subject-centred methods of their teaching. They are obliged to make everything relevant to pupils' lives, to stress sociological and historical contexts in all areas, to emphasise practical skills and applications, and to introduce large tracts of course and project work into assessments. All of this cannot but militate against the coherent organisation and structure inherent in an academic discipline, and which one would have expected at least some 16 year olds to have been introduced to.

I wrote to Professor Shock about his remarks, and he was kind enough to tell me in reply that his main concern in making them was 'to wake people up in the universities to the nature of the problems they will soon be facing'. One might have thought that a Committee of Vice-Chancellors and Principals would have spoken out against the changes in academic standards that were being wrought with the introduction of the GCSE, and would have hinted, perhaps, that the universities should consider setting their own entrance examinations if GCSE stage 1 and the rumoured stage 2, which will replace A-Levels, could not be relied on. So far, though, the Vice-Chancellors have not seen their duty in this way. But however they eventually see their role in relation to the defence of academic standards, it is not clear that we need all acquiesce in the GCSE approach to education in the way the Vice-Chancellors are apparently doing at the moment. Those of us in schools and universities and elsewhere who do care for academic standards and the virtues of traditional learning, and who see secondary education in terms of the disciplined initiation of pupils into worthwhile and structured forms of knowledge might put our minds to devising some other form of examination, which has it as its aim to test such things, and to encourage pupils and teachers to cherish the values inherent in them.

7. MULTICULTURAL EDUCATION[1]

David E. Cooper

The theme of multiculturalism throbs insistently through the official publications relating to the GCSE: in the Secretary of State's paper *Better Schools*: 'all pupils need to ... acquire a positive attitude towards the variety of ethnic groups within British Society';[2] in the GCSE 'General Criteria': 'The value to all candidates of incorporating material which reflects (ethnic) diversity should be recognised';[3] and in almost all of the National Criteria for particular subjects. A main aim of Geography, for example, is to 'encourage an understanding of different ... cultures within our own Society';[4] while the Social Sciences syllabus is to 'encourage cross-cultural study as a method and means of promoting awareness of cultural differences between and within societies'.[5] Similar remarks, predictably, populate the Religious Studies, English and History syllabuses.

Until the GCSE is properly underway, one cannot be certain how loudly this theme will emerge in actual performance. But three considerations suggest that this multicultural emphasis will deeply affect, or even transform, the teaching of many subjects, as well as much else that goes on in schools. Firstly, the GCSE proposals should be taken in conjunction with those of the Swann Committee Report, *Education for All*, which were endorsed by Sir Keith Joseph and by substantial sections of the educational profession. The official style and trappings of the Report should not disguise its radical content: 'There is ... no area of the curriculum which will not be enhanced significantly in educational terms by the incorporation of a pluralist perspective.' And in *all* schools 'multicultural understanding has ... to permeate all aspects of a school's work.'⁶ In Religious Studies 'diversity (is to) be celebrated'; in English, ethnic minority languages are to be included in 'the mainstream curriculum'; special training centres are to be set up to examine 'the implications of cultural diversity for "all white" schools' – and so on.⁷

Secondly, there is the evidence from those schools and those LEAs which have, as it were, jumped the gun and already adopted robust multicultural programmes. The ransacking of libraries for 'Eurocentric' literature, Brent's 'full training in racism awareness' for all its employees, and the ILEA 'teaching package' *Auschwitz – Today's Racism* belong, one hopes, to the 'unacceptable face' of the movement. However, one fears that this face will not be shy to expose itself further once official priority is given to the aims which such practices purport to serve.

Finally, it is not only in the general rhetoric, but also in the detailed proposals of the GCSE syllabuses, that the multicultural theme is heard. In Mode I Religious Studies, pupils are not required to study Christianity and may instead cover up to three other religions practiced in this country. In 'recognition ... of the richness of cultural diversity', English students need no longer read works from 'what is traditionally regarded as the canon of English literature'.⁸ And some History syllabuses are virtually denuded of British history, with 'key issues' such as race relations filling the space.

In short, projections based on the enthusiastic reception of Swann, on current practice in some LEAs, and on particular GCSE syllabus plans, suggest that the multicultural urge may indeed transform what happens in our schools.

It is generally agreed that there has been a major shift in the idea of a multicultural education. Time was when it was considered as primarily directed towards ethnic minority children – as a means of fostering their cultural heritages and of mitigating an 'underachievement' deemed to be due, in part, to their having to acquire an 'alien' culture. Although these aims have not disappeared, the contemporary emphasis is on multicultural education for *all* children – those in 'all white' schools included. In the words of Swann, it is an 'education for all'.

What are the main aims of this 'new' multiculturalism supposed to be? One of them, to which I shall return later, is, of course, to 'combat' racism. But the aim to which most attention is given – at least in the 'official' literature – is an educational one. As Swann puts it: multicultural education is 'justifiable, and indeed essential, on straightforward educational grounds ... (it is) essentially synonymous with a good and relevant education for life in the modern world'.[9]

But what are these 'educational grounds'? I detect two arguments. The first is that pupils will be 'enriched' through their vicarious encounters with other cultures. Without further support, however, this consideration does nothing to warrant a curriculum in which prominent attention is given to ethnic minority cultures. Let us grant, with reservations, that pupils are 'enriched' by encounters with other cultures. This leaves it wide open as to *which* cultures they should study. Life, especially school life, is too short to study them all. Now why should it be assumed that an encounter with Sikhism rather than Taoism, with Caribbean literature rather than Russian, with African philosophy rather than Ancient Greek,[10] should be the more 'enriching'? People should indeed acquaint themselves with the most 'enriching' cultures; but it is absurdly optimistic to assume that these are the ones conveniently found in certain parts of London, Birmingham, or Bradford. Someone will reply that their being found here is what makes all the difference. But this is to shift to ground that has nothing to do with 'enrichment'. There may be good reasons for giving special attention to what is here and now: but only someone of temporary and myopic vision can think that the here and now must have most to contribute to the 'enrichment' of understanding, sensibility and imagination – in short, to educational 'enrichment'.

The second educational argument is the one contained in Swann's reference to a 'relevant education for life in the modern world', and in the *Better Schools'* reference to 'preparing pupils for an ethnically mixed society'.[11] Made explicit, the argument is this: a good education reflects, and prepares for living in, society as it actually is. Ours is a multicultural society, hence, a good education will be one 'permeated' by a multicultural perspective.

Crucial here is that cliché of contemporary discussion, 'ours is a multicultural society'. As John Rex points out, this is 'said ... too glibly .... Britain is not a multicultural society in the sense that Quebec or Brussels is.'[12] Cultural divisions in Britain, unlike Canada, are constitutionally irrelevant; so that ours is not a multicultural society in the sense that it is, say, a democratic society. Nor, one might add, in the sense that it is a technological society: for no one can think that all aspects of everyone's social life are indelibly stamped by the presence of ethnic minorities in the way they are by the technological nature of work and leisure.

Just such a reason is also needed if the point about education's 'reflecting' actual society is to have the desired implication. Naturally, education should reflect that there are ethnic minorities in the sense of informing pupils about this, and about the problems faced by these minorities. But, equally, education should reflect, in this sense, that Britain has such-and-such an industrial or legal system. There is a huge gap, however, between this and the Swann proclamation that every area of the curriculum must 'reflect' society by incorporating a multicultural perspective. An unfortunate effect of glib slogans like 'ours is a multicultural society' is that people seem to feel no need to provide such reasons – no obligation to *argue* why the multicultural aspects of our society should be of so much greater educational moment than its many other striking features.

There is, says John Rex, a better way of reading 'ours is a multicultural society': namely as a *commitment* 'to fostering minority languages and cultures and (to) regard(ing) them ... as a source of enrichment'.[13] But so construed, the slogan does nothing to *support* the multiculturals' conclusion, since it already has this conclusion built into it. If the overhaul of History, English *et al* is to be *justified* by an appeal to the multicultural nature of our society, that appeal must be more than a mere restatement of a commitment to this overhaul.

The main educational arguments for a radically multicultural curriculum are, then, fallacious or circular. But could someone come up with some better arguments? Possibly, but at this point I want to urge some reasons why such a curriculum could be positively *counter*-educational.

As several contributors to this volume note, many GCSE syllabuses require or encourage pupils to cover extremely broad areas. One reason for this breadth is that there is no longer to be concentration on the 'narrowly Anglo or Eurocentric'. World Studies is the most striking instance of expansion, but Religious Studies also deserves special mention. Not only are pupils to study a number of religious figures and doctrines, and a variety of moral and social questions, but they are encouraged to do so in connection with no less than three religions. (No more than three, lest 'depth of understanding' is lost!) It is small wonder that critics refer to a 'Cook's tour' approach. The objection is not simply 'Too much too soon': for, as the experienced traveller knows, not only is it essential to limit the mileage if one is properly to appreciate anything, but appreciation presupposes an understanding which is brought *to* the places and people one encounters. This understanding – be it of architecture, religious devotion, or political systems – cannot be got from whirlwind tours. Naturally there is much to learn from 'other cultures', but initially at least there is necessarily an element of translation, into one's own terms, of what these cultures have to offer. Understanding of how 'they' think, build, worship and organise themselves must be by way of comparison and contrast with how 'we' do these things. No one, schoolchild or professional anthropo- logist, can grasp the exotic – or even recognise it *as* exotic – except in relation to what he is already familiar with.

It is no use objecting here that, while understanding must begin somewhere, it is 'imperialist' or 'Anglocentric' to begin with 'our' traditions not 'theirs'. For this implies that traditions are *options* to which one is first and foremost introduced at school. In fact they engulf the child – at home, in the streets, in front of the television – from the moment he begins his odyssey as a social and linguistic being. To borrow Hans-Georg Gadamer's striking metaphor, under- standing of others requires a 'fusion of horizons' – theirs with ours: and ours are ones whose limits are provisionally determined much more by the lives we live than by the lessons taught us in the classroom. Swann tells us that we must replace 'an anachronistically Anglocentric view of the world ... by syllabuses which are global in their perspective'.[14] If this simply meant, for example, that children should not be brought up on G.A. Henty and other chauvinistic historians, no one would demur – and no one has demurred for a very long time. But if it means, as it seems to, that History teaching need not begin with and continue to emphasise the past of our own country, it is absurd. Educationally absurd, that is, and not simply because of the natural, and eminently healthy, special interest which people have in their own past. The reason is that, if History is to impart understanding at all, the emphasis must be somewhere, and not dissipated every-where. And one then wonders how to take seriously the suggestion that the emphasis should not be on the past and traditions which anyway impinge upon us, and mould us, as participants in the society whose past and traditions these are.

My further worries about the counter-educational ten-dencies of multiculturalism revolve around an ideological *diktat* to be found in most of the supporting literature, including the GCSE 'General Criteria' and the Swann Report. This is to the effect that, not only shall teachers and pupils approach matters pluralistically, but that they shall adopt a 'positive attitude' towards, 'respect', and 'celebrate' the religious, ethical and literary diversity resulting from the presence of ethnic minorities. This is not empty rhetoric: as can be gauged from the fact that there are plenty of cultures, past and present, towards which pupils and teachers are *not* encouraged to take a 'positive' attitude: Edwardian England, say, or contemporary California. Nor, it seems, do the values of country squires or 'Sloane rangers' figure among those whose diversity we are sup-posed to 'celebrate'.

Now there is much which may concern people about the intrusion of such an ideological element. There is the fear, for example, that it may serve as a green light to the more obsessive enthusiasts of multiculturalism, whose practices can already be observed in Brent and elsewhere, and whose

educational blueprints are no secret.[15] After all, it is not
only the teacher who fails to emphasise cultural diversity
who will stand condemned. So will those who, in the eyes of
the watchdogs (the LEA 'advisers', say), fail to instil a
sufficiently 'celebratory' attitude towards it.

But the main educational worry about the *diktat* must be
with its abrogation of that critical judgement which traditionally it has been the aim of liberal education to promote.
To be sure, there are plenty of references in the GCSE
criteria to encouraging 'rational criticism' or 'objective
assessment'. But it is difficult to reconcile these with the
pre-emptive decision that the arts, mores or whatever of
minority cultures are all to be regarded 'positively'. What,
for example, is the real meaning of the insistence in the
Religious Studies syllabus that pupils be tested for their
ability to 'support an opinion coherently', when it has just
been laid down that no religious viewpoints may be
regarded as 'invalid'? What 'objective assessment', one
wonders, has gone into the ruling that religious diversity in
a country is to be applauded? Is it supposed to be
self-evident to the critical mind that, despite Northern
Ireland, Sri Lanka, or the Lebanon, such diversity must be
'celebrated'?

One should also ask, parenthetically, whether this *a
priori* accentuation of the positive in all aspects of ethnic
cultures is compatible with the accompanying emphasis on
'respect'. As John Harris puts the question, is it 'in reality
more respectful to protect or to challenge the beliefs and
practices of those cultures with which we disagree'?[16]

It is not only the ideological *diktat* which is at odds with a
sincere concern to develop critical judgement. Indeed, the
very idea of a multicultural education, with its demand for
the study of many traditions in many fields, is barely
compatible with that concern. Given the 'Cook's tour'

through so many cultures which is proposed, it may be just as well, I suppose, that critical judgement is *not* to be encouraged. For we should scarcely admire the sight of scantily informed pupils sounding off on the virtues or vices of whatever they have so fleetingly touched upon. Real critical judgement rests upon, and is directed towards, what is genuinely understood. Otherwise it is blabber: something which is not made the more attractive coming from the mouths of babes. The breadth demanded in a multicultural syllabus necessarily carries with it the elimination of any truly detailed content with which pupils must get to grips. Yet it is precisely in getting to such grips that critical judgement is flexed. That the problem here is compounded, not cured, by alternative emphases on 'method', 'course assessment' and 'dialogue with texts' is well-argued by several articles in this book – those by Worthen and Deuchar, for example. Perhaps Sophocles' Tiresias exaggerated in calling the power of judgement Man's greatest gift: but it may be the greatest one education has to confer. And it is this gift which the ideology of multiculturalism threatens to withdraw.

These remarks prompt a few words, of a more philosophical kind, on the topic of *relativism*. For it appears that some people positively welcome the abrogation of critical judgement, seeing it as the consequence of realising that values and standards are 'culturally relative'. Many critics have, fairly enough, made logical sport of relativist slogans such as 'All cultures are inherently equal'.[17] It is reported that the Brent Multicultural Adviser became angry when it was pointed out to him that, by this slogan, Afrikaaner culture is on a part with Indian, and he insisted that teachers knew clearly enough what was meant.[18] But it is not all clear: for once one admits that some cultures are more equal than others, one is conceding that there are, after all, criteria for judging cultures. Then there is the problem, familiar since Socrates' criticism of the arch-relativist Protagoras, of the status of the relativist's own claims. Multiculturalists of a relativist bent seem peculiarly resistant to according a merely relative validity to their own principles.

But I shall not pursue this sport, primarily because I accept the possibility, at least, of versions of relativism that present less easy targets. Instead I shall suggest, on two grounds, that even a plausible relativism would not provide the support usually supposed for a multiculturalist overhaul of our education. Multiculturalism may need relativism, but relativism does not necessarily need it.

I take the relativist idea to be that cultures may be so different that, since there are no 'trans-cultural' criteria, evaluation must be invidiously based on the values drawn from *within* one or other of the cultures. Such a relativist walks a tightrope – for the cultures he has in mind must be sufficiently different for the standards of one to get no purchase, as it were, on the other: yet sufficiently similar for them to be mutually intelligible – for otherwise we could not even recognise that their values conflict. Too often he falls off the tightrope. Either the other society he describes sounds too alien for us to identify what its values and standards are, or it sounds sufficiently like our own for our standards to be applicable when evaluating their ways. But let us concede, at least for the sake of argument, that some cultures – Samurai Japan, say, or the Azande – are at the required distance from our own.

The trouble is that if *these* are at the right distance, then the ethnic minority cultures in contemporary Britain certainly are *not* – either from each other or from the so-called 'dominant white culture'. The life of British Afro-Caribbeans, for instance, has massively more in common

with that of the majority than with that of their distant
African ancestors. Black or white, we work in the same
industries, participate in the same institutions, enjoy the
same laws, watch the same television – and so on. The
premise the relativist needs – that a culture's practices be
too alien to our own for anything but invidious, parochial
comparison – is completely missing in such cases. And
because it is missing, it is absurd to demand that the
standards accepted in one culture in our society be
suspended in mid-air so as not to touch upon those of
others. (Actually the whole talk of there being different
cultures in our society seriously misleads here.) We cannot,
for example, proclaim a sincere commitment to equality of
rights for the two sexes and then refrain, as some bid us do,
from passing judgement on certain Islamic attitudes to
women. To do so would imply that Moslems living in the
country constitute an hermetically sealed society whose
form of life is too tangential to our own for our principles to
get any grip. This is not to suggest, incidentally, that we ride
roughshod over Moslem sensibilities in this area, in the way
that ILEA promoters of 'positive images' of lesbianism in
the school seem happy to do.

My second point is that, even if the ethnic cultures in
Britain fitted the relativist's bill better than they do, it
would remain unclear why members of the 'dominant'
culture should suspend or trim their values and commit-
ments. It is unclear, that is, why the absence of an
ahistorical, trans-cultural criterion of evaluation should be a
good reason for any culture to alter its ways and standards.
The views of Richard Rorty are relevant here. He first
quotes, with approval, another author's reference to

> those loyalties and convictions whose moral force consists
> partly in the fact that living by them is inseparable from
> understanding ourselves as the particular people we are.

Rorty then adds:

> ... there is no 'ground' for such loyalties and convictions
> save the fact that the beliefs and desires and emotions which
> buttress them (are) those ... of the group with which we
> identify.

And this, he says, is ground enough.[19]

Now this is relativism – but of a kind deeply antithetical
to any multiculturalism which desires the 'loyalties and
convictions' of one culture to be diluted simply because they
are not those of other cultures. It is antithetical, for
example, to the Secondary Examinations Council's demand
that the traditional study of English be savaged so as to
'meet the requirements for ethnic ... balance'; or to a
new-fangled 'History for all' which will ignore, when it does
not decry, the heroes, movements and deeds – including
those of our 'imperial' past – which have forged the history
of which we are the bearers. More generally, it is inimical to
the onslaught on 'Eurocentrism'; for this is but a pejorative
label for that European heritage – from classical times,
through Renaissance, Reformation, Enlightenment and
Romanticism, to Modernism and the Age of Science – in
terms of which educated Westerners (and not just these)
define themselves. And, one might add, in terms of which
alone they are *then* able to learn from, and appreciate, what
other heritages may also have to offer.

Finally, I would like to question the popular view that a
multicultural education serves as an important weapon in
'the battle against racism'. For some this is the main
consideration – to the extent indeed that the very term
'multicultural' is criticised for distracting away from the
'basic issues of power and oppression in society'.[20]

I shall be discussing anti-racism in some reasonable and
honourable sense of the expression: and not that inverted

racism which, with the help of disingenuous definitions, some people have twisted the expression into naming. (A prime example of disingenuous definition is the one which builds the idea of power into the meaning of 'racism', in an attempt to secure the result that only whites can be racist. A comic effect is that Nazis ceased to be racist after May 1945; and a less comic one is that there can be *no* racist element in attacks on, say, Indians by people from other minority groups.) It is not useful, I think, to attempt an exact definition of 'racism', but I take the central ingredient to be that of advantaging and disadvantaging people on the basis of their ethnic membership.[21] So our question concerns the role of multicultural education in combating such practices and the attitudes which underlie them. I have two main doubts about that role.

Echoing dozens of others, Lord Swann writes: 'Prejudice ... is the child of ignorance, and who better than teachers to dispel such ignorance.'[22] No doubt particular prejudices can on occasions be eliminated through an appreciation of the facts. But I see no reason to think that, in general, prejudice is a function of ignorance. For just what is it, one asks, of which prejudiced whites are ignorant? One reads of people who are alleged to believe that all blacks are irredeemably promiscuous, dirty or whatever: but even if these people are not wholly caricatures, they can form only a tiny fraction of those who, according to anti-racists, are guilty of prejudice. So one asks again, what exactly is it that we have to learn, such that, having learned it, our prejudice will evaporate? There is, to be sure, an unlimited amount to learn about ethnic minorities – their music, their food, their customs, and so on. But why would gathering such information have even a tendency to stamp out antipathy towards, say, Pakistanis? We might, I suppose, mean by 'ignorance' that lack of living acquaintance with others which only day-to-

day contact can make good. But, if so, the answer to Lord
Swann's question 'who better than teachers to dispel such
ignorance?' is not the one he wants to give. For even the
most inspired teacher could do next to nothing by way of
providing those experiences of living among others which
ignorance, in this sense, is contrasted with.

The doctrine of prejudice as the child of ignorance
manifests, in fact, a naive Enlightenment, or perhaps
technological, faith in the power of factual knowledge,
which events of the last two centuries should surely have
eroded. Were the Russians and Austrians who turned on
the Jews at the end of the last century more ignorant than
their more tolerant grandparents? Are people in countries
like France, where colour prejudice has been less striking
than elsewhere, simply more knowledgeable? Could their
knowing something which others do not be even *part* of the
explanation? It is, incidentally, merely bad history to cite,
as so many do in this connection, the crazy racist 'science' of
Nazi Germany. For, of course, anti-semitism had already
taken root long before these theoretical rationalisations,
which were anyway ignored or quietly derided by most
Nazis, including Hitler himself. Nor, of course, was it the
demise of this 'science' after 1945 which played any
noticeable role in the subsequent erosion of anti-semitism.

My second worry is akin to the familiar fear of a 'white
backlash' against over-zealous anti-racist programmes. Not
that this fear should be taken lightly, for it should occasion
no surprise if people become angry at some of what goes on
under the anti-racist banner – the persecution of individuals
like Miss McGoldrick; the brouhah about a 'blackboard',
'Baa-baa-black-sheep' and other 'racist' language; and at
publications which, but for their being directed against
whites, would be prosecuted under our Race Relations
legislation.

But my worry is a distinct and, in the long term, more serious one. The *ideal* of anyone who wants an end to racism should surely be that of a colour-blind society: one in which a person's colour or race is no more salient, no more to be remarked upon and taken account of, than his height or tone of voice. What is needed is, almost literally, a loss of perception. For whatever the more particular explanations of prejudice in a society, its precondition is that racial difference should stand out in relief. (The upsurge of anti-semitism in turn-of-the century Vienna and Prague was largely the result of an influx of orthodox Jews, fleeing the *pogroms*, who were so much more *obviously* Jewish – in dress, customs, *etc.*, – than those already settled in the cities.) Yet it is just this precondition whose continued existence will be guaranteed by an educational policy which, in classroom or playground, perpetually emphasises matters of race and colour.[23]

One secondary school declares its policy thus:

> *No* incident, however apparently trivial, should be ignored, and *every* opportunity should be taken to teach positively against racism .... A record of *any* incident, *however small* ... should be completed in the *Serious* Incident form in the section entitled 'action taken'.[24]

There is fanaticism here, for no school which took this policy literally could pay balanced attention to the many other aspects of children's behaviour which require censure and correction. More to the present point, such policies – especially when yoked with a curricular stress on ethnic problems as the 'key issues' to be studied – can only sharpen that acute perception of racial differences on which racism feeds. This tends to be masked, unfortunately, by the focus of many anti-racists on 'unconscious racism'. This is not an easy notion to make sense of, but it is best understood, perhaps, as the unthinking and habitual manifestation of attitudes which are generated from a vivid, and perfectly conscious, perception of racial differences. If so, 'unconscious racism', like the racism of which it is an extension, presupposes that salience of race which we should be trying to dim down, not to highlight.

What I have been saying would indeed be depressing if it meant that education as such, as distinct from a robustly multiculturalist one, must be ineffective in combating prejudice. But it does not mean this. Unpalatable as it may be to some, it has always been among the less well-educated – whether in Hitler's Germany, South Africa, or post-war Britain – that racial prejudice has flourished most. This is not because the better-educated have known something, had some information, about racial issues and differences which others have not. Rather, the product of a traditional, humane and liberal education – the educated mind – is one which, at its best, is as unreceptive to racism as to any other kind of unreasonable discrimination and lack of sensitivity. An acquaintance with the best that has been written, thought and enacted is not easily transformed into a sympathy with what is worst in human behaviour. What is depressing, naturally, is that the educated mind is precisely that which is currently under threat.

This book is published in the knowledge that the arrival and continued existence of the GCSE are settled. What is not settled, however, is the degree to which practice will accord with the proposals promulgated in the National Criteria and other documents. In particular, it is not settled whether the multiculturalist rhetoric of those documents will be fully translated into reality. It can still be hoped, therefore, that the work of translation will be suspended – at least until the proponents of multiculturalism do better than hitherto in justifying the refurbishing of our education, and in answering criticisms of the kinds I have expressed.

8. SKILL, FUNCTION, AND CULTURE

Hywel Williams

Educational reformers popularly understood to be on the Right speak of the need to relate the world of work to that of the school. In so doing they urge a greater degree of 'vocationalism' in British education and a return to, and expansion of, those 'skills' necessary for our survival in the international market-place.

Educational reformers equally popularly understood to be on the Left also use the notion of a 'skill', but in a different context. The progressivist burghers of Islington or Haringey direct their gazes away from the stock-markets of New York, London and Tokyo in order to peddle their own brand of social control and cultural determinism. Their talk of 'life-skills' similarly subordinates the fugitive deliverances of the understanding to a rationalist scheme of social amelioration and proposes the substitution of one approved code of behaviour for another.

The notion of a 'skill' unites, therefore, these otherwise profoundly opposed bodies of opinion but there is obviously something unsatisfactory about a word and an idea which can be used so evasively and ubiquitously in order to achieve widely differing effects of exhortation. 'Words', wrote Thomas Hobbes over three centuries ago, 'are wise men's counters, they do but reckon with them, but they are the money of fools.' Our linguistic confusion with respect to 'skill' reflects historical and social confusions and complexities of a peculiarly English kind. This essay addresses these confusions and tries to observe Hobbes' dictum. It directs the reader away from the 'surface grammar' of the word 'skill' and towards the contexts and assumptions within which it operates.

Many European languages seek to record a difference between two types of understanding which might be variously categorised as being the difference between external 'technical' knowledge and internal empathy – between the detached observation that *x* is the case and the claim born out of suffering, joy or fear that one has experienced and therefore knows that *x* is the case. G.W.F. von Hegel in developing this distinction characterised it as the difference between *Vernunft* (Reason) and *Verstand* (Understanding). French, of course, records the difference between *savoir* and *connaître*; Italian observes the distinction between *sapere* and *conoscere*, while German distinguishes between *wissen* and *verstehen*. While all these cases may differ from each other in their application they illustrate a readiness to accord a different, and possibly higher, status to the kind of knowledge English refers to as 'intuitive'. The carefully judged, demarcatory nature of the word is a significant truth and doubtless an illustration of tenacious English pragmatism and empiricism. It is, however, equally revealing that the English distinction between knowing and understanding is far from clear and certainly does not provide us with an exact parallel to the German, French and Italian examples. The difference between 'knowing' Samuel and 'understanding' him only become obvious when the two verbs are juxtaposed in this way. I might, unknown to you, have been making a very 'high' claim when I say initially, and without qualification, that 'I know Samuel'. When I wish to make a claim about Samuel's writings I can either say that I know or understand the works of S.T. Coleridge. The latter is doutbless the stronger (and more cocksure) claim but I could have arrived at the same destination by using 'know' in an expansive sense.

English as a language, therefore, may be peculiarly receptive to the claim that the 'technical' language of 'knowing how' is inseparable from the language of 'knowing that' and that, therefore, the notion of a 'skill' is no neutral one, easily separable from more contentious matters. The decision as to which skills we wish to acquire, our beneficient acquiescence in the skills bequeathed to us socially and individually, our repugnance at other skills; none of these are matters of mere technical proficiency, they all raise the question of value, and show that 'skilful' is as ambiguous word as 'good'.

Certain skills can only be acquired in certain cultures. The idea of a modern English university education in the Humanities is overwhelmingly bound up with the invention of History and English as disciplines of thought. They have both developed certain, highly marketable skills, have both operated very effectively as the channels for doctrine and ideology for the secularised intelligentsia in a post-Christian age, and are both marked by the circumstances of their birth. Many historians, when asked to reflect on their activities, would assent to a version of Rankeanism. However difficult to achieve, they would still see von Ranke's aim of seeing the past *'wie es eigentlich geswesen'* as a relevant aim. Questions of bias, detachment and objectivity would doubtless arise but, the professoriate would argue, our professional skills are designed to exclude such challenges to our integrity. The claim, however, that one should study the past 'for its own sake' is by no means as self-evident as this version of events suggests. Ranke's own version of 'historicism', it is now clear, relied upon a combination of modified German liberal nationalism along with a reliance upon the more individualistic and mystical elements within the religious traditions of German Pietism. This was the context within which Ranke and his disciples developed their formidable powers of scholarship in the German universities of the nineteenth century. The aspiration to see each epoch as equal under God was, to them, no bland piece of professionalism. The unreflective habits of contemporary historical Rankeans wedded to a skill devoid of content may be a form not only of intellectual sloth but also of unexamined, and therefore doubly dangerous, prejudice and assumption.

The study of English as a formally separated area of study developed later in England than did the study of History although, in effect, the two had been sharing the same areas of concern since at least the 1880s. In both cases the first great expansion in staff and student numbers in schools and universities took place in the years after the First World War and produced figures who were quick-witted enough to exploit the contemporary malaise. Men such as I.A. Richards, William Empson and F.R. Leavis acquired their authority with an ease which seems astonishing until one remembers that they were operating within a scholarly post-war vacuum and were able to capitalise upon the steadily diminishing authority of the Classics as a normative and stablising centre of *humanitas*. The Cambridge technique of 'close criticism' (a 'skill' if there ever was one) was in this respect a highly gnostic device designed for the initiate readership. In its formulated desire to see the 'object' in itself as it really existed, it shared more than a vocabulary and an aspiration with the Historical School: it also shared an opportunity for the dissemination of values and the creation of influence.

Mediaeval studies of a literary, linguistic and historical nature have provided impressive examples of this dissemination in twentieth century England. The Mediaeval

England and Europe of the Chester-Bellocian fantasy and its organic harmony of faith and life which was used to provide a corrective to the Edwardian plutocracy is a well known example. Chester scholarship, however, although reticent behind the claim to be studying the past for its own sake can also be shown to be responding to contemporary and practical imperatives. No body of knowledge in the modern Acadamy can claim more formidable forensic skills than that of the Mediaevalist and this has not prevented the practitioners of these skills from contributing implicitly to a debate on the nature of the Modern State. In reading Professor Sir Ernest Barker and J. N. Figgis on the origins of mediaeval political thought, Professor Sir Maurice Powcke and Professor Sir Richard Southern on the modalities of the religious life and its relationship to political power and practice, we read a series of debates whose terms have been set unavoidably by the two central experiences of England in the twentieth century: the decline of Christanity and the failure of the centralised liberal State.

No commentator upon the human past can avoid the resonance of that which has been given him within his own experience; it is a precondition of his success as a commentator that he should acknowledge and explore the resonance. Hegel once wrote that the philosopher could not 'leap over Rhodes', he could only describe that which was given. The truth of the remark applies to all humane study which involves acts of interpretation, and the recognition of its truth, far from foreclosing the options, in fact releases one through self-consciousness to a more effective exploration of those options. We do well to recall here the full force of J. M. Keynes' famous remark that those who declare themselves to be the slaves of no theory are usually the unwitting slaves of an outmoded theory. The theoretical implications of an education of 'skills' are, likewise, not

easily avoided. A culture as understandably hostile as ours
to the claims of theory and, for the same reasons, to
étatisme, may well have to come to the difficult acknow-
ledgement that the recovered notion of a 'core' curriculum
of linguistic, historical and scientific/technological skills
depends upon an equally recovered notion of citizenship.
This is not to be taken as a plea to return to Whig ideas of
development and progress in our classrooms and lecture-
halls. That particular and theoretical understanding of
ourselves, although still surprisingly dominant in our
narrowly constitutional as opposed to our political histories,
reflected advantages no longer enjoyed by ourselves. A
wide, intelligent, and discriminating reading public, a State
minimal enough to avoid calumny, and a coherent, unfrivolous governing class; these conditions no longer obtain in
contemporary Britain. By contrast, we sustain a stultifying
bureaucracy, frustratingly impervious to reform, and divorced, in education as elsewhere, from the vivifying power
of practice and direct responsibility. Venerable, humanist
notions of knowledge as *bildung* (self-knowledge) and of
the process of learning as justifying itself have been taken
over by, and subsumed to, the self-interest of a caste of
'educators'. In the process the vocabulary of Erasmus
looses its significance. In looking beyond such a caste-
interest we should recognise that an education of 'skills' of
any kind requires a cultural context of human aspiration
and value. The reforms of Sir Keith Joseph and of Mr Baker
require the posing of the question: What does it mean to be
a citizen of the Nation-State in late twentieth and early
twenty-first Centuries?

A skill is an abridgement, and the ability both to transmit
it and to be educated within it is not easily divorced from
the continuum of human behaviour and expectation, in
short the tradition, which puts flesh and sinews upon the

wraith of the skill. When we withhold our highest admira-
tion from the skilful pasticheur, the irritatingly self-
conscious virtuoso, a Lizst or a Meyerbeer in music, a
Greuze or a Boucher in painting, we do so on account of a
just reservation about the limits of mere virtuosity. Their
ability to extend the grammar of a tradition of which they
are doubtless a part is, we feel, limited by the external
nature of their relationship towards that tradition. Having
mastered the short-cuts, they have lost sight of the
landscape of those masters within which context alone those
short-cuts originally made any sense. Their grammar
thereby descends into a mere technique and becomes a
grammar of impoverished Esperanto. The virtuosity of a
Bernini, a Mozart or a Wagner is a far different matter since
in those cases the technical mastery of a skill is achieved
with an ease and grandeur of effect which makes a nonsense
of the conventional and pallid distinction between 'Art' and
'Craft'. Baldinucci, in his life of Bernini published in 1682,
two years after the death of the Master, recounts the
affecting story of the aged sculptor labouring without rest
on the marble and saying, when implored to take a rest by
his assistants in the workshop: 'Let me stay here, for I have
fallen in love with it.' Bernini's staggering skill as a cutter of
marble cannot be distinguished from the lessons he learned
from his investigation of Hellenistic torsos in the Vatican,
the harmonious High Renaissance groupings of Raphael
and Michelangelo, Caravaggio's studies of realism in
extremity and from his experience, we are told, in placing
his own leg into the flames in order to observe his agony.

Bernini's relationship to his marble is akin to the variety
of conversations and engagements which are pursued as a
means of understanding and discovery by the members of a
coherent and mature culture. For a participant within such a
series of conversations to ask for an epitome of them which

he could, as it were, take away with him and impart as a
lesson or a skill to someone who had not been a participant
would be to display a failure to understand the nature of the
proceeding. This is one reason why the notion of a life-skill
to which I referred at the beginning of this essay is so
implausible: it abstracts the idea of a skill from the context
which gives it life and, in so doing, also contributes towards
the misunderstanding of what it means to be absorbed
within a process of education. In learning the grammar of
moral behaviour, as indeed in learning the grammar of any
language, the more assured our behaviour will be and the
less inclined will we be to resort to grammatical rules or
generalisations and summaries of behaviour. Our command
of the landscape (although never complete, since we are
participants in a process which can never be brought to an
exhaustive conclusion) will allow us to dispense with the
misleading abridgements, the hastily contrived skills of the
ideological Ordnance Survey map. Even to raise the
question of a skill, therefore, and of how it might be taught,
is to recognise implicitly the extent to which an entire
culture has broken down.

Recognitions of a political and administrative kind
confront us at this point. Although both the present
Secretary of State for Education and Science and his
predecessor have been fertile innovators there has been a
marked disparity between the world of their discussion
documents and the inertia and perversity, as Sir Keith
Joseph characterised it memorably, of organised bodies of
educational opinion in the LEAs, the teaching unions and
elsewhere. Since it has been one of the main thrusts of the
argument of this essay that reforms even of a superficially
'technical' kind involve revised assumptions of a theoretical
and structural kind this disparity should not surprise us. In
order to cope with the disparity we have, over the past year

or so, witnessed the paradox of a Conservative administration centralising its powers, and it is difficult to avoid the conclusion that further measures of a centralising kind will be necessary in the future in state education.

Although conventional wisdom of a Whigish kind decrees that we should congratulate ourselves on having avoided an English 1789 the results of that avoidance have not been uniformly happy. We live in a State of the ancien régime whose cantankerous and oppositional *philosophes* occupy positions of decentralised and subsidised power. Systematic and original criticism of the system's monopolistic abuses is, therefore, a task of great and increasing difficulty. In lacking the more benign effects of centralisation which were attendant upon the events of 1789 in other parts of Europe, the nineteenth century State in England failed to provide a view of itself as an educational instrument and enabler. We have only experienced the malign effects of centralisation under such members of the educational high-priesthood as the late Mr Anthony Crossland and Mrs Shirley Williams (the Madame Eglantine, perhaps, to his Saint-Just). The development of a view of what political education should consist in is surely one of those contexts referred to earlier and within which the recovery of skills can flourish. An inspection of Advanced Level syllabuses in Political Studies reveals how much needs to be re-thought or swept away: historically unsophisticated constitutional study, tendentious and intellectually undemanding material abound.

It is difficult, admittedly, in these matters not to fall victim to the inflation of expectations characteristic of life lived under the aegis of the Welfare State. Since we spend such vast amounts of money on 'education' we feel correspondingly affronted when our desired and, of course, variable and conflicting goods fail to be delivered. We make a superficial equation between increased expenditure and higher standards when the whole of the post-war experience of this country is contrary to that assumption. Where, as in the present case, issues of national culture arise as an element in our educational thought the need is for a different kind of intellectual preparation.

Corelli Barnett in his recently published *The Audit of War*, gives us a stridently argued critique of the historical and contemporary defects in English education. The book is a well documented and in many ways appalling indictment of British industrial performance during the Second World War. In his accompanying excursions into social and intellectual history the author repeatedly indicts the teachings of the public schools, of Oxford and of Cambridge, for having been responsible for a climate of opinion hostile towards entrepreneurial businessmanship. The literary, humanistic, classical bias of English education at its highest levels are therefore held responsible for this country's century-long industrial decline.

How plausible is this claim? One's initial reaction is that it is likely to flatter the pedagogic influence of the schoolmaster and don that soft-headedness and sloth are surely far more convincing explanations of decline than the supposed academicism of *'luxe, calme et volupté'*. While one welcomes the issue of a national culture being broached it is regrettable that the need for an ideology of excellence should be raised in such a simple-minded way. It is difficult to see why a literary education, for example, should disqualify one from making rational judgements about an industrial enterprise. Barnett's remarks on the baneful influence of Wordsworth and Coleridge in this context are a good example of the Higher Silliness in action. The same undiscriminating appetite leads him to quote in two different contexts, and at length, the same passage from Dr Arnold's writings which discusses the relative claims of gentlemanly conduct, Christian ethics and of scholarship. For Barnett the text is a crucial one in demonstrating the ease with which ethical high-mindedness triumphed over bloody-minded competitiveness. The fact that the passage is in fact as hostile to the claims of 'pure' understanding, of the untrammelled intelligence pursuing 'academically' the truth 'for its own sake' as is Barnett himself is likely to make us pause. When we reflect on the ties between a skill and a national culture we do well to remember that the Bismarckian nation-state which, in its centralising, managerial efficiency, is very much the Barnett ideal, was also the first European Welfare State. Therein, 'skills' of a technical and industrial kind of a very high order flourished alongside social ideologies of a crude and dangerous kind. The works of Treitschke and the phenomenon of 'Social Darwinism' are both relevant examples of the dangers of an advanced system of technical education which is not co-ordinated within a wider scheme of values.

The desirability of a skill, therefore, presupposes a wider pattern of expectations, abilities and choices. The skills involved in the reading of *Paradise Lost* are not readily available to the reader in a culture which sees Biblical and classical allusions as elements to be patiently uncovered rather than as second nature. The ability to read in context is a result of emancipation from the insistent tyrannies of a modish present, and issues in a recognition of the miraculous 'otherness' of the object of study, the pastness of the past, the objectivity of the work of art. Hence the difference between the merely alert observer and the educated investigator who, although in similarly unchartered depths, knows how to frame the relevant and fruitful question.

The grammar of a skill, after all, like the grammar of any language embodies beliefs and attitudes. Such a grammar does not provide 'thought' with its outward expression, its

cloak as it were; rather is the language equivalent to the
'thought', the link between them being necessary and not
adventitious. This is one reason why Ezra Pound defined
poetry as 'that which gets lost in translation'. The techniques and skills of a Virgil, a Dante or a Pope are transmuted
with such difficulty from one language to another precisely
because of the differing social and cultural matrices within
which their languages were formed.

Skills therefore differ. This is why we wish to discriminate
between them, rejecting some (those of the back-street
abortionist or of the bank robber) and desiring others
(those of the speaker of Russian or of the concert pianist).
This discrimination is invariably an evaluative matter and its
ability to illuminate will vary. The fact that we choose to
make a distinction between theoretical and practical skills,
for example, says more about the way we understand
ourselves than it does about any possible 'subject' of
discourse. Matthew Arnold's contrast between the 'Heb-
raist' who lives by the Law and the 'Hellenist' who lives by
the Spirit, tells us more about Victorian Hellenism and
Arnold's place within it than it does about either St. Paul or
Plato. Not only the desirability of a skill but also the whole
notion of what constitutes a skill owes much to the context
of a culture. The principles of Newtonian science and those
of Einsteinian relativity theory both produced skills whose
values were strictly in line with their cultures and not easily
spearable from them. For Newton himself his skills were a
propadeutic not merely to the world of the Royal Society
and of the Deists but also to the world of alchemy, prophecy
and millenarianism. Their transformation into Baconian
precepts was no obvious and straightforward matter.
Similarly, and perhaps more obviously, the principles of
Einstein's understanding come to us out of a world, that of
fin de siécle Vienna, which was obsessed with multiple

perspective, ambiguity and cultural dissolution. The novels of Robert Musil, the paintings of Klimt and the music of Mahler are so many facets of the same concern that issued in Einstein's reformulated physics.

The continued efficacy of a skill depends upon the maintained vitality of its relationship to a larger body of knowledge. Knowledge of all kinds involves communication between the generations, and where that conversation becomes febrile, pedantic, formulaic or in other ways strained and arid, skills, and much else besides are lost. The inculcation of a certain kind of dominant skill may indeed result in an unhealthy lack of originality and a consequent failure to revise the categories of understanding. Schools of thought and of expression as their visions wane and their arteries harden in the second and third generations after the progenitors, provide us with abundant examples of this process. Marx disavowing the 'Marxists' on his deathbed, the tenets of Classicism, Romanticism, Modernism, Realism, Freudianism, Ignatious Loyola, Stravinsky and Schoenberg, Adam Smith and Voltaire, turned into tabulated 'Schools of Thought': all of these illustrate the tendency at work. Skills, when creative, are not static but dynamic concepts continuously evaluated by those who have to use them. In the long and unresolved debate on whether education reflects or creates the society by which it is surrounded, schools and universities reverberate with the echoes of that revision. Only the fact of that continuous revision and not its empirical details may be predicted, for, as the structure of scientific revolutions illustrates, the hitherto 'theoretical' may suddenly and surprisingly become the overwhelmingly contemporary and 'practical'.

The long rationalist shadow of Plato falls over any discussion of skill, education and citizenship. Plato's analogy between the skills displayed by the captain of a ship and those needed by the rulers of a State illustrate a common rationalist fallacy that the understanding of a process involves the abstraction of certain essential principles from that process. The essential features of the analogy are those involving aim, purpose, or direction and choice of one to whom we entrust the journey. Those features which limit the analogy, however, remind us of the truth that a dispute about the direction of a sea, or any other, voyage is not a dispute about values, as disputes about citizenship very often are. The *technē* of a statesman engages us in debate precisely because the skill is implicated in ethical questions which are contestable.

As the process of educational reform gathers momentum we need to think of how we may reform the lamentable and intellectually second-rate 'specialism' of our schools. The problem is a widely observed one and has been made more acute by the GCSE's flawed concentration on subjects at the expense of the connections which may subsist between them. There is here a failure to think creatively and a lack of integration which lead to the widespread phenomenon of what one might call 'label-ism': the belief that identifying and understanding an object, belief or event is the same thing as characterising it under a general name. Such a characterisation is usually a convenient excuse for ceasing to think.

No one should delude himself, therefore, that an emphasis on educational skills is a safely 'vocational' and pragmatically convenient way of attaining consensus in a faction-ridden world, where ignorant armies clash repeatedly in a dark conceptual night. Skills require a social ideology. They do so because, like all constructed accounts of what constitutes 'knowledge', they are an aspect and a consequence of social order. The liberal tradition in English political thought has been so dominant since the age of

Locke that we find it difficult to give an account of the State
in any terms other than those of manipulation and of willed
contrivance. A moment's reflection, however, on the
matter may cause us to revise our assumptions. Notions
such as those of mercy, charity, justice, skill, theory,
practice, righteousness and dispassion do not lie 'out there'
in Nature, as it were, waiting to be picked up and used.
They are constructs which only become possible within the
life of groups and of institutions, and their work is related to
the maintenance of social order. These constructs are not,
as the liberal political tradition maintains, freely created by
rational egotists beyond or anterior to the institutional
world. Secular political institutions are no different from
religious ones in that they are both defined by belief and
should not be understood as the mere instruments of a
manipulative will. They offer the possibility of shared
experience, knowledge and principles as means of unification. Far from relativising knowledge this view of its
ideological and social function rescues it from the arbitrari-
ness which plagues the liberal individualist's solitary
account of how a man 'chooses' his values.

If the foregoing account is a correct one then the
opportunities for original thought within the world of the
independent boarding-school is now and will be greater
than at any other time since the early nineteenth century.
Here are institutions whose cognitive aims are pursued
within the matrices of a diverse and all-embracing institutional order and whose creative energies can be astonishingly ramified. They have the ability and the resources to
experiment with a more variable, sophisticated and internally more coherent series of syllabuses. In doing so they
may recover that centrality of vision – the sense of serving
the interests of an entire national society – which was such a
striking feature of their institutional history in the

nineteenth century. They contain within themselves, at their best, that blend of the individual with the communal which has been the hallmark of the great movements of reform in European history from the followers of St. Francis to the Young Hegelians and the Victorian Evangelicals.

When scepticism and triviality are actively promoted by those institutions which once operated as powerful centralising norms of sanity and reason, a visionary touch is needed. It is not unreasonable to expect the public school tradition to supply that correction and that vision. Indeed, it is in that tradition's own best interests that it should be central and not marginal to our national life. The consequences of the diffused voluntarism which characterised educational advance in the nineteenth century have been varied. Those countries which developed a clearer notion than ourselves of the educative role of the State are now more prosperous than ourselves. The French Revolution created universal free state schooling and Prussia was the first nation to establish elementary education. In Japan 95% of all pupils remain in their schools beyond the school leaving age and some 80% do so in the United States. British secondary education, in contrast, retains only 15% of its pupils after O-Level. In our own nineteenth century experience a variegated, highly individual, and self-reliant pattern of institutional foundation and aspiration reflected a nation fertile of ideas and innovative of spirit within the context of an unfrivolous governing class. Sadly, these are advantages we no longer enjoy.

Those who twit the present Government with inconsistency in its educational policies – which appear to involve both administrative decentralisation and doctrinal unification – require a longer perspective. The legacy we have been given is that of a voluntarism which has run out of ideological steam and which needs to be revived. The centralising advantages enjoyed by other countries only became apparent to us when our institutions became ossified and when that which had been a source of strength became one of weakness. Voluntarism of endeavour had been so successful because, far from operating within a moral vacuum of arbitrarily chosen freedom, it had in fact presupposed a morality of law and convention. For the early Victorians, revealed religion had been the source of these norms. The mid- and late-Victorian intelligentsia, the generations of Ruskin, George Eliot, Gosse and Leslie Stephen, substituted for this an intense moral zealotry, a concern with the question of the extent to which 'morality' may be regarded as justifying itself. The compulsive and self-regarding dissidence of the generation following theirs, and inevitably associated with the name of 'Bloomsbury', failed to supply a consensus. Therein the cult of the private flourished.

There is no paradox involved in the recognition that the recovery from such a collapse entails the diffusion of power only within the context of externally defined standards. As this essay has sought to demonstrate, such communal standards and categories of knowledge, citizenship and virtue are not easily avoided. They are the soil within which our highest aspirations may be rooted.

9. THE POLITICISATION OF EDUCATION

Joanna North

In his essay in this book on Multicultural Education, David Cooper describes how education is now infused with the aims and values of multiculturalism. The GCSE national criteria require that all subjects should encourage in children an appreciation of ethnic minority cultures. In this respect, and in the fact that the aim of this new emphasis is to combat 'racism', the education system has become politicised – education has become an instrument whereby political awareness may be fostered and certain social and political ends achieved.

In fact, education has for some time – certainly since the early 1970s – been used in this way. Sociologists of education have for many years criticised schooling as a process whereby social inequality is maintained and reinforced:

> Education creates the myth that those at the top deserve their power and privilege, that they have achieved their status on merit and that those at the bottom have only themselves to blame. In this way the educational system reduces the discontent that a hierarchy of wealth, power and prestige tends to produce.[1]

With such a view of education being taught to teachers in training colleges for so many years, it is hardly surprising that some teachers and many educational advisers have attempted to use education to redress the evils they see in society.

The incorporation of a multicultural perspective into the curriculum is only one in a long line of fashionable causes. Anti-racism, anti-sexism, anti-heterosexism, World Studies and peace studies are some of the other subjects which have been introduced into schools in the last few years, with a view to using the classroom for the purpose of initiating widespread social and political change. Many of these new initiatives are taught at secondary level as Mode 3 courses, devised and assessed entirely by individual teachers and subject to little, if any, external control. At the present time more than 4,000 Mode 3 courses exist throughout the country. No proposals have been made which would monitor their content and educational value more closely, although under the GCSE all such courses (like any other) have to conform to the national criteria.

Some educational writers have expressed fears that education is now feeling the influence of the 'New Right', as a result of an ideological swing away from the progressive ideals of the 1960s and 1970s.[2] The facts of the matter, however, suggest a different interpretation. If one examines the national and subject-specific criteria, and if one studies some of the proposed syllabuses for the GCSE, it appears that many of the leftist ways of thinking have been incorporated within the new system. It seems to be accepted that education can and should attempt to address itself to political issues, and that through an appreciation of social, political, economic and environmental topics children should be encouraged to find their own answers to questions which in the past were left to adults to pursue.

The commitment to this view of education is expressed clearly in the national criteria, which specify those conditions to which all subjects and syllabuses must conform. For example:

In devising syllabuses and setting question papers Examining Groups should bear in mind the linguistic and cultural diversity and society. The value to all candidates of incorporating material which reflects this diversity should be recognised.[3]

All syllabuses should be designed to help candidates to understand the subject's relevance to other areas of study and its relevance to the candidate's own life. Awareness of economic, political, social and environmental factors relevant to the subject should be encouraged wherever appropriate. Questions seeking to test this awareness should be in the context of the subject concerned and not be independent of it.[4]

Within the subject-specific criteria we find evidence of politicisation in a number of subject areas. In Science, for example, 15% of the total marks are to be allocated to the candidate's appreciation of the social, economic and environmental implications of the applications of science. In Geography we find the claim that the subject is a valuable medium for 'education in a social context', in which children may be taught to appreciate the 'existence of marked contrasts in the level of economic and technological development between and within nations'. One of the guidelines for the drawing up of syllabuses in Geography is that all courses should include components which deal with the 'geographical aspects of important social and environmental issues such as the problems and opportunities of development in less affluent nations'. If the candidate is to achieve a Grade C he must be able to show his understanding of geographical ideas in a range of situations – 'social, economic, political and environmental' – and show 'an increased comprehension of judgements made on economic, political, environmental and social issues'. Statements such as these illustrate the extent to which real education is being destroyed through the politicisation of the curriculum. Instead of regarding subjects such as Science and Geography as of educational value *in their own right*, we are told to assess the merits of particular subjects in terms of their capacity to serve external ends. Education is now regarded as a 'valuable medium' for the inculcation of certain social and political attitudes.

Social Sciences are, of course, prime targets for politicisation – candidates must be taught to appreciate the awareness of cultural differences within and between societies, and to develop 'a critical awareness of social, economic and political arrangements'. The content of Social Science courses must include an examination of the 'process of income and wealth generation and distribution', and 'the implications of gender for society and for the individual'. Such issues we should expect to find in a Social Science course, but even Computer Studies cannot be studied without the candidate being taught to 'develop an awareness of ethical, social, economic and political consequences of the use of computers for individuals, organisations and society'.

Practically every subject, therefore, has some broadly political component. Some people may not see this fact as especially worrying. On the face of it the references to 'social, political, economic and environmental issues' are couched in the most innocuous of terms – in terms which would allow all points of view to be acknowledged. However, the sad truth of the matter is that those who will actually *welcome* the incorporation of such issues into the curriculum are likely to have their own political axe to grind. All the available evidence suggests that the points of view which children are to be 'encouraged' to 'appreciate' will in practice tend to be those of a left-wing nature. This is true despite the fact that the national criteria stipulate that 'Every possible effort must be made to ensure that syllabuses and examinations are free of political, ethnic, gender and other forms of bias'. It is because the education system has for so long been regarded by the self-appointed 'experts' as one which generates and maintains inequality and disadvantage – benefiting children who are from well-off, middle-class homes – that the requirement that bias be avoided may be read as a call for the adoption of left-wing approaches. If existing curricula and examinations are seen as already biased towards 'right-wing' values and viewpoints, the introduction of explicitly left-wing issues and values may be carried out in the name of balance and fairness.

The formal requirements of the GCSE examination and syllabuses encourage and reinforce the view that the classroom is an appropriate place in which to combat certain 'evils' within society. Thus every child in almost every subject will be required at some time to address himself to political issues, and be judged in terms of his ideological fitness. This latest attempt at social engineering should immediately be opposed by all those who care about genuine education. But I suspect that few parents perceive the nature or the extent of the danger. In the rest of this essay, therefore, I will attempt to show how two particular subjects have become politicised, and how the politicisation in question involves an attempt to manoeuvre pupils towards a left-wing attitude. Before I begin, however, it will be helpful to say something about the nature of indoctrination. Once the chief characteristics of indoctrination have been identified it will be easier to pinpoint the ways in which certain school subjects are now open to manipulation.

In a pamphlet entitled *Education and Indoctrination*,

published in 1985,[5] a number of characteristics of indoctrination are identified. Three of these will be of particular
interest in what follows:
(1) Conclusions are foregone. Evidence of foregone conclusions may be found when loaded questions, loaded references and loaded vocabulary are used. An example of a
loaded question, which might be found in many sociology
examinations, is 'How does schooling reproduce social
inequality?' Loaded questions are phrased in such a way as
to presuppose certain answers to other 'hidden' questions.
In this case, the question presupposes an affirmative answer
to the question '*Does* schooling reproduce social inequality?' The first question is loaded, containing the assumption
that schooling *does* reproduce social inequality as a foregone conclusion.
(2) The conclusions reflect a certain unity of outlook which
is based in a particular emotional or political attitude. The
claim that schooling reproduces social inequality, for
example, is usually put forward by someone who accepts a
particular political viewpoint, one which is critical of
'capitalist society' and its 'bourgeois' institutions. Such a
person is likely to embrace a cluster of causes, some of
which – anti-racism, anti-sexism and anti-heterosexism –
have already been mentioned, but which also include
anti-Americanism and a hostility to nuclear power and
nuclear weapons.
(3) The conclusions are 'premises to action'. The proponent
of anti-racism, anti-sexism and so on is an advocate of
political action. His beliefs are not merely theorectical but
suggest and recommend certain courses of political action.
Indoctrinatory education will frequently involve, therefore,
children being encouraged to participate in political activities.
    By contrast, genuine education involves a respect for

truth and an open-minded approach to all questions. No conclusions are foregone, and no particular political attitudes are presupposed. As the authors of *Education and Indoctrination* say:

> part of the aim of education has been to promote rational discussion, and respect for truth, so that when the mind closes upon its conclusions it does so neither impetuously nor prematurely, but in full consciousness of what it is being asked to believe, and in such a way as to remain responsive to argument and evidence.[6]

Let us look now at the teaching of Geography. As in many other subjects there has been a gradual move, in the last 15-20 years, away from the acquisition of factual knowledge. This move has been supported by an attitude which regards the learning of facts as a redundant form of learning. In the case of Geography such an attitude is reinforced by a view of the world as undergoing change at an increasingly rapid pace. One may question the self-evident character of such a view; nevertheless, it is brought forward as a reason for abandoning a whole tradition in Geography teaching:

> The increasingly rapid pace of political, social, economic and even environmental change is quickly rendering information about places redundant.[7]

Why should it be so important *now* that we alter the way in which subjects such as Geography are taught? The view of the world which lies behind the new conception of the subject-matter of Geography is that of a constantly-changing, highly-complex, interconnected and integrated network of relationships. Once such a picture has been accepted it is easy to argue that certain teaching methods – predominantly holistic in character – should be employed in tackling the subject. It is no use to argue that the world is still relatively stable, or at least stable in most areas of the globe, and that children might still profit from the study of cereal production, rainfall levels, weather and climate variations, and the principal natural resources of each country. Such a view is no longer fashionable, and we are compelled to bow down to those who require us to consider the 'interrelationship and interaction between people and their environments', the 'control and management of resources', the 'problems and opportunities for development in less affluent nations', and the 'United Kingdom's relationships, for example in trade and industry, with wider groupings of nations such as the EEC'.[8] As a result of the new Geography, children may well develop a sensitive appreciation of the world's eco-system, but remain completely ignorant as to the principal capitals of the world or the names of oceans and seas and where they are located.

Of course, it is not merely a change in the way the world is perceived that is responsible for the new emphases in Geography teaching. A number of factors are responsible, and each has contributed to the altered character of the subject. In the first place, the new approach gives full rein to the idea of child-centred education which has been the norm since the early 1970s. It is no longer the *content* of a subject which is of importance but the *process* or learning *experience*. Factual learning and recall are no longer desirable, for such approaches to education are considered unfair and disadvantageous to certain children. This insistence on process rather than product is enshrined in the national criteria for Geography, one of which states a necessary element of content to be 'a first hand study of a small area, preferably the student's home area, which provides not only opportunity for direct experiential learning but also a basis for comparative work on a scale which is readily comprehensible'.

A second factor lying behind the new Geography is the acceptance of the notion of 'values education'. Fully in keeping with the philosophy of child-centredness, relevance and the stress on the *experience* of learning, children are to be taught not to acquire factual knowledge, but to develop a sensitive appreciation of the different values which people place on particular issues. They are encouraged to develop empathy for other people in situations different from their own. This is supposed to be educationally enriching, and also to help the child become a more mature, more fully developed individual. Values education is thus as much a *moral* issue as an educational one in the strict sense.

The national criteria favour this approach to the teaching of Geography. The subject should be used in order to:

encourage an appreciation of the significance of the attitudes and values of those who make decisions about the management of the environment and the use of terrestrial space;

and to:

develop awareness of the contrasting opportunities and constraints facing people living in different places under different physical and human conditions.

This sensitivity is not something that can be directly tested in the examination. Nevertheless, the national criteria state that it should be encouraged.

The national criteria say that one of the uses to which Geography may be put is that of providing 'a perspective in which [students] can place local, national and international events and enable them to function more effectively as individuals and as members of society'. The GCSE *Geogra-*

phy Guide for Teachers produced jointly by the SEC and
the Open University in 1986 is more explicit about the role
of values education in Geography:

> Values education in geography is more than the develop-
> ment of an appreciation of the part played by the values and
> attitudes of people or groups in geographical situations .... It
> provides us with opportunities to assist students to develop
> their own self-concepts, emotions, values, decision and
> action skills in a geographical context.

Approaching a subject in this way obviously has its
dangers. It will be difficult in practice to draw a clear
dividing line between values education and values *inculcation*, and teachers will have to take great care that they do
not set aside the aim of instilling knowledge, in favour of
the aim of inducing ideological conformity. In other words
there remains a worry that indoctrination will occur, and
this worry becomes greater when one examines some of the
teaching materials which are likely to be used. I shall discuss
these materials in detail later on. For the moment it will
suffice to point out that some teachers will positively
welcome the new approach to geography teaching precisely
because it *does* offer opportunities for politicising the
curriculum. F. Slater, in his article 'Literacy, Numeracy and
Graphicacy in Geographical Education', says that:

> it is at these growing edges that geography's role in
> developing political literacy ... coincides with some of the
> more educational concerns for encouraging political under-
> standing and educating affectively as well as cognitively.[9]

I have said that a particular vision of the world as a
rapidly changing integrated system, the philosophy of
child-centred and experiential education, and the emphasis
on values education are three of the main factors which lie

behind the new orientation in Geography teaching. Each of these, I believe, has played its part in the politicisation of the curriculum, and, as a result, has made it easier for indoctrination to take the place of education. In the first place the picture of the world as a holistic system in which each element is connected to every other and cannot be seen in isolation, has encouraged the abandonment of the pursuit of factual knowledge which in the past was a crucial aspect of Geography. Instead of introducing children to a body of knowledge and teaching them facts about the world, they are now introduced to 'areas of discussion' and are taught to appreciate and indulge in the mere expression of opinion. The curriculum is open to indoctrination in that there are fewer tangible areas of factual information to be tackled: they have been replaced by topics and areas of study where only contestable (but foregone) conclusions can provide anything looking like a coherent structure. The notion of an objective truth, which can be easily grasped through studying the facts of any particular situation, has been replaced by the aim of developing 'sensitive appreciation' and 'empathic understanding' – abilities which, in the wrong hands, are easily turned into the instruments of political conscription.

The emphasis on experiential and child-centred education has moreover encouraged the view that children have a unique contribution to make to every subject, a contribution which requires them to make their own decisions about social and political issues. It is my belief that it is wrong to encourage children to take an active role of this kind. At best the child will make ill-informed decisions and develop sympathetic attitudes towards those people who can most easily be sentimentally portrayed. At worst, the child will be open to indoctrination of the most unscrupulous kind, to a degree that was never possible when teachers concentrated on teaching them facts about the world. Finally, values education is often explicitly advocated by those who favour the politicisation of the curriculum, and who wish to make children 'politically literate' and able and willing to take an active role in opposing what their radical teachers describe as injustice and oppression.

In some schools children are taught Geography under other names – World Studies, Global Education or Education for International Understanding. This is particularly the case where schools offer Mode 3 courses. World Studies is far more political in tone than Geography as it has traditionally been taught. But it is precisely because World Studies explicitly incorporates the three features discussed above – the holistic view of the world, the importance of experiential learning, and the stress on values education – that a World Studies approach or slant to the Geography curriculum is likely to prove popular. Indeed the advocates of World Studies are keen to incorporate its aims and values into *all* subjects, and not just into Geography – just as the advocates of Multicultural Education wish to see all subjects infused with the spirit of multiculturalism. It is therefore worth spending some time looking at the nature of World Studies and the materials which World Studies teachers are encouraged to use.

In 1986 the Southern Examining Group (SEG) drew up a proposal for a Mode 3 GCSE course in World Studies. The holistic picture of the world is introduced on the first page:

> World Studies is a recognition that on our earth we all have a future which is dependent on a common natural environment, humanity, economy and spirituality. Changes at any one level affect the whole, as the processes and factors influencing them work as an interrelated and interdependent system.

A child-centred approach and an emphasis on values education are also stressed early on:

> It is important that recognition be given to the value of students' existing attitudes and feelings as starting points from which further understanding can be developed. Students should be encouraged to develop empathy for other people whatever their age, class, creed, ethnicity, gender, ideology, language, nationality and race.

The holistic vision, the importance of experiential learning and the role of values education are reiterated in the aims of the syllabus. For example:

> To develop:
>
> An understanding of the systemic nature of the world.
>
> An awareness and understanding of the complex interrelationships within environmental systems and the place of the human species within those systems.
>
> An awareness of the holistic concept of health as being the fusion of the bodily, emotional, intellectual and spiritual dimensions of a person living in harmonious relationship with the planet.
>
> Consciousness of personal perspective and of how all perspectives are influenced by a range of factors such as age, class, creed, culture, ethnicity, gender, ideology, language, nationality and race.
>
> An awareness and appreciation of a range of cultures and of what humanity holds in common.
>
> Heightened levels of self-awareness and self-esteem.

Some of the aims are explicitly political in tone:

To promote:

A concern for justice, human rights and responsibilities.

An understanding of the dynamics of conflict and coopera-
tion from the personal to global levels.

An understanding of the sources, distribution and exercise
of power.

An understanding of and an enhanced capacity to participate in political and other decision-making processes.

The content of the proposed World Studies course is set
out in the form of a diagram, reproduced in *Fig*. 1. A glance
at some of the topics will show the contentious and
politicised nature of such courses: Over-development;
Under-development; North-South poverty and affluence;
power; violence; justice; equality; neo-colonialism; peace
within; interpersonal peace; international peace; origins of
conflict; arms race; cold war; protest; freedom fighting;
terrorism; oppression; persecution; prejudice; sexism; racism; minorities. Indeed, almost every fashionable left-wing
cause is reflected in the proposed content. Although
lip-service is paid to the importance of maintaining balance
and of drawing from established disciplines 'the rigorous
procedures for the appraisal of evidence from a variety of
sources and points of view', when one comes to look at the
materials which are available for teachers of World Studies
courses it soon becomes apparent that the orientation of
World Studies courses is predominantly leftist in character.

Thus, the economic relation which exists between the
'North' and the 'South' is invariably regarded as unjust and
exploitative. The 'rich' North – i.e. North America and the
countries in Western Europe – are to blame for maintaining
an oppressive system which benefits the well-off at the

Fig.1: Content Model for SEG GCSE Mode 3 syllabus in World Studies

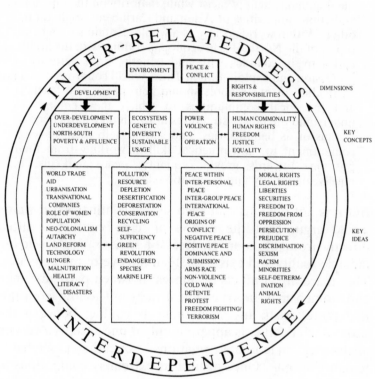

expense of the poor. This unjust system is seen as exacerbated by the build-up of arms and military expansion. Robin Richardson, for many years an adviser in Multicultural Education to Berkshire County Council and one of the leading lights of the World Studies network, makes this message explicit:

Our society contains conflicts of interest between social classes, between the sexes, between generations, between the dominant, mainly racist white majority on the one hand and ethnic minorities of Asian and Caribbean origin on the other. Within world society as a whole, Britain's ruling elite is part of the North: it is in economic conflict with the South, and actively colludes with and benefits from patterns of repression and exploitation in Third World countries .... The curriculum of our schools should help pupils and teachers and the local communities to which they belong, to understand the power structures in which they participate as victims or as beneficiaries, and should help them develop commitment to, and practical skill in working from their positions towards greater equality, peace and justice, locally, nationally and internationally.[10]

But it is not obvious that such severe conflicts exist. Many would argue that the notion of 'class conflict' – lifted directly from Marxian analyses of society – refers to no tangible reality and exists solely in the eye of the beholder. That there are conflicts of interest between particular men and women may be true, but it does not follow from this that there exists any such thing as conflict between the *sexes*. Such conflict is apparent only if one accepts a certain analysis of male/female relations – one that is explicitly feminist in tone. Once again it is extremely contentious to say that the majority of white people are racist. One has only to compare the record of British society for its tolerance and respect for other cultures with the extreme intolerance displayed by some minority groups for one another, to see that an alternative viewpoint is at least possible. And the claim that the North is operating a system of exploitation in which the countries in the South are robbed of their wealth and resources is also questionable: is it not rather the case that the system of international trade operates for the benefit of *both* parties, and that without it developing countries would be much worse off than now? Whatever the truth of these claims it is surely true that there are alternative points of view, and that such points of view must be taken seriously and given proper attention. Unfortunately, in the case of World Studies, 'alternative' viewpoints – i.e. those which defend the value of international trade and the role of multinational companies in the Third World, for example – are nowhere treated with serious consideration. It is taken for granted at the very beginning of inquiry that certain systems and relations are unjust and exploitative. The fact that this is so indicates the indoctrinatory nature of World Studies as a subject. For its major premise – the unjust distribution of goods – is also a foregone conclusion.

The second characteristic of indoctrination which was mentioned earlier – that the conclusions reflect a particular political attitude, which is unified around a cluster of beliefs and ideals which share a similar character – is also apparent from an examination of the GCSE World Studies syllabus and its typical teaching materials. The political attitude of one who accepts that the system of international trade is exploitative and oppressive can adapt itself easily to incorporate other views which depend upon similar assumptions: the belief that nuclear power and nuclear weapons are evil and that it is the West's reliance upon nuclear weapons which is likely to precipitate a Third World War, for example; or the view that the IRA and the Tamil separatists are 'freedom fighters' with justice on their side, rather than terrorists, determined to subdue their opponents through force and fear.

World Studies advocates frequently claim that traditional teaching methods and traditional subjects are 'ethnocentric', 'North-biased' and 'stereotyped'. The educational values of truth and objectivity are dismissed as 'rigid',

(2) A 'wheelchair project' in which 'a small group of girls wheeled one of their number into city shops, restaurants, etc., to assess the facilities available from the point of view of a disabled person'.

(3) A 'Community against the Bomb' group, which involved children in drawing up petitions.[13]

The use of such 'involvement projects' is just one way in which 'political literacy' – in effect, encouraging children to become political activists – may be heightened in the classroom. It is indicative of that third feature of indoctrination mentioned earlier – that the conclusions of the arguments behind World Studies are 'premises to action'. Children are encouraged to participate in political activities, and as we can see from the third example given above, these activities tend to be those which reflect one particular political hue.

The philosophy underlying World Studies, and the politicisation of the curriculum which it involves, may not as yet have penetrated into all Geography courses and syllabuses. But, if we return for a moment to Stewart Deuchar's argument, concerning the extent to which the values of the Schools History Project have entered into mainstream History teaching, we are likely to conclude that a similar process is occurring in the case of Geography. World Studies courses have been taught in schools, sometimes under other names, for a number of years, and the traditional curriculum has had to bow to pressures from the radical left, whose views on education have for some time been standard in many areas of curriculum and syllabus design. As Keith Orrell says in his essay on Geography:

> When, a few years ago, the task of devising the National Criteria began, it was taking place in a changing curriculum environment in which doubts were already being expressed about the value of the new 'scientific' geography in school.

The *new*, new geographies – behavioural, welfare, humanistic and radical geographies – were beginning to be seen as having much to contribute to the students' education.[14]

I have already suggested that the national criteria for GCSE Geography allow for, and to some extent encourage, the development of radical initiatives in the teaching of Geography. Some of the topics are almost identical to those favoured by the World Studies advocates: the existence of multicultural communities and societies; the contrast in levels of development between and within nations; environmental deterioration; and those social, economic, political and environmental questions to which geographical concepts and ideas are applicable. When Sir Keith Joseph addressed members of the Geographical Association with the words:

And how adequate is the political understanding achieved through geographical studies? Do teachers take full advantage of their opportunity to give attention to a wide range of political processes at local, national and international level?[15]

he was surely unaware of the dangers of advocating teaching for 'political literacy'.

Another subject which is increasing in popularity is that of Integrated Humanities. At present Integrated Humanities courses at GCSE level are on offer from the Midland Examining Group (MEG), the Northern Examining Association (NEA), and the Southern Examining Group (SEG), which between them comprise seventeen examination boards. This subject is as woolly-minded in its presentation, and as vaguely-defined, as World Studies. And it leans, once more, on the child-centred, values-oriented philosophy which supports the new Geography. Indeed, Integrated Humanities – lacking any coherent content of its own – is 'reactionary', 'sterile' and 'bourgeois'. Armed with views such as these the World Studies teacher enters the fray, determined to counter the reactionary nature of traditional school teaching. He will find that there is no shortage of teaching materials with which to carry out his task. For many years various charitable organisations have been developing books, films and other materials for use in his courses. Oxfam and Christian Aid are perhaps the most well-known of these organisations, but there are many others: Action Aid; Unite and Understand; War on Want; and the Voluntary Service Overseas (VSO). Many religious organisations are also active in promoting World Studies and development education: the British Council of Churches; the Catholic Fund for Overseas Development (CAFOD); the Christian Education Movement; the World Development Action Campaign of the Methodist Church. Other, more explicitly political, organisations which produce material that crops up on recommended lists for teachers include: All London Teachers Against Racism and Fascism (ALTARF); Campaign Against the Arms Trade (CAAT); the Institute of Race Relations; the National Association for Multi-Racial Education; the Peace Education Project; Third World First; and, of course, the Campaign for Nuclear Disarmament (CND).

All these organisations differ in their aims, and not all are equally guilty in producing biased and politically indoctrinatory material. Nevertheless, a significant number of these organisations and a considerable amount of the material which they produce give cause for concern.[11] The Christian Education Movement produces a topic folder entitled 'Our World', in which the rich North's responsibility for the poverty of the Third World is simply assumed without argument:

> For our economic privilege we want them to be not rich and powerful enough to compete with us or to threaten us, and our commerce and industry try to keep it that way.[12]

Asking 'What causes poverty?' the pamphlet gives the answer as 'the greed of the rich'. We are told that if real change is to take place the rich must first lose their wealth and power.

Christian Aid produces a booklet called 'Caring about Trading' in which it is said:

> Many meetings are held between rich and poor countries to try to find fairer trading agreements. These are not very successful because rich countries are not usually very generous.

Christian Aid's booklet 'Desert, Drought and Danger' provides the following reading for children at harvest festival time:

> It's a crazy world:
> millions of pounds are spent defending people from
> their apparent enemies.
> Their real killers,
> disease, hunger and poverty,
> continue to murder with impunity.

Such material is highly tendentious and misleading, to say the least.

In keeping with the stress on child-centred education the proponents of World Studies encourage the use of 'involvement projects' in schools. David Selby refers to a number of projects which were used as a part of a World Studies course taught at a Midlands comprehensive school. These included:

(1) Raising money for local and international charities.

the skills-based examination *par excellence*. The SEG's syllabus, published in 1986, provides a good illustration of the intellectual vacuousness which is the unmistakable preliminary to indoctrination.

The 'subject' is defined broadly as the 'exploration of the human condition', and the Integrated Studies teacher is free to draw upon a vast array of disciplines in providing some content for the course: Economics; Geography; History; Religious Education; Political Studies; Psychology; Sociology; Craft; Design and Technology; 'Personal Relationships Education'(!); the Expressive Arts; and the Sciences – all are possible candidates.

What then are the aims of Integrated Humanities? Once again, the wording is extremely vague:

> An understanding of human societies which will enable informed and reasoned judgements to be made about significant contemporary issues.

> An understanding of the social and cultural context of life in modern society ...

> An awareness of the meaning and diversity of human values, a sensitivity and empathy towards people living within different spatial, temporal, socio-economic and cultural contexts, and thus a preparation for responsible participation in a multicultural society.

> Social, economic and political literacy ....

Despite the breadth of the aims one can already sense the political agenda lying beneath it, and the values which the teacher is expected to encourage in his pupils. The examination itself, as one would expect, consists largely of coursework assessment and project work, all to be assessed internally. 40% of the total marks go towards four pieces of coursework, 30% of the marks are allocated to the assessment of a candidate's folder of 'personal research work' concerning 'some clearly formulated question or problem', and the remaining 30% covers assignments completed under 'controlled conditions'. The nature of these 'controlled conditions' is not clearly revealed. There is to be some time limit certainly, but it is unclear what are the 'stimulus materials' which are to be used, nor is it clear how little 'teacher guidance' is to be allowed.

Each school following the SEG syllabus has to select five topics which the pupils are to study. The syllabus offers 24 examples, but schools are free to choose others, provided that they satisfy the general requirements for subject content. For example, a topic must incorporate four 'contextual levels' and four 'conceptual areas'. The topic must relate to the following contexts: the individual; the community; the national scale; and the global or international level. The four conceptual areas are as follows: power and distribution (the political dimension); ideas and ideologies (the moral dimension); space (the geographical dimension); and continuity and change (the historical dimension). The topics suggested in the syllabus include the following: peace and conflict; law and order; the mass media; race and culture; gender inequalities; unity and division; beliefs and values; political movements; world interdependence; prejudice; human rights; wealth and poverty. Once again, the political agenda is blatant.

The NEA's Integrated Humanities syllabus is more detailed in its description of the course content. The details of the 15 suggested topics are set out in Appendix 1 at the end of this book. A careful examination of these will show, once again, the scope for indoctrination and bias inherent in the issues chosen. For example, under 'Law and Order'

students are to look at 'the extent to which the law affects
the individual's freedom of action', 'conflict between
minority group norms and the law', and 'the social versus
hereditary basis of criminality'. In studying the 'Mass
Media' students are to consider 'the extent to which the
mass media in the United Kingdom are free from political
control'. The topic of Education offers candidates the
opportunity to consider 'the criteria and the responsibility
for determining the curriculum, e.g. multicultural, anti-
racist, anti-sexist approaches' and 'the relationship between
social class, educational opportunity and life chances'.
Topic number eight aims to provide students with the ability
to recognise examples of 'Persecution and Prejudice', and
they are expected 'to demonstrate an understanding of [the]
sliding scale of persecution ... and to appreciate how one
step on it provides a threshold for the next'. Students will
therefore examine the 'universality of prejudice' in its
different forms: xenophobia; segregation; scapegoatism;
victimisation; ostracism; bigotry; endogamy; paranoia;
stereotyping; snobbery; elitism and so on. Areas of persecution are given as follows: race; politics; religion; gender;
class; and physical handicap. It is assumed throughout that
the preference for one's own race or culture is in all cases a
matter of prejudice, and that there is widespread persecution of people on grounds of gender, class and physical
handicap.

A few more examples from the NEA's syllabus will
suffice to show the politically biased nature of its content.
The causes of inequality given in topic number nine are
'possession of wealth and power', 'control of resources',
'access to education', 'trading patterns', 'colonialism' and
'external control of resources, (e.g. by multinational companies)'. It is unlikely that points of view which do not
automatically equate inequality with injustice will be

considered with any seriousness under this topic. But it is clearly a contentious claim to say that inequality is the result of the possession of wealth, or to say that multinational companies are responsible for maintaining situations of inequality. There is not even the smallest pretence here at providing a balanced and unbiased approach. Again, under the heading of 'War' we do not find the view that nuclear weapons are a means of preventing and controlling war; rather, the 'reaction to real or suspected threat' and a 'state of war-readiness' are listed as two of the *roots* of war.

In considering the *nature* of the politicisation inherent in such syllabuses, similar considerations to those raised earlier in connection with World Studies apply. Where a subject is new and where that subject is concerned to promote political literacy and encourage empathy in the pupils, it is more likely than not to gravitate towards those resources and materials which have flourished in the last ten years or so – materials which in many cases are clearly biased and deliberately indoctrinatory. The study of peace and conflict will typically involve extensive use of CND and anti-nuclear literature; law and order is likely to be treated in ways which, in the present climate, are unsympathetic to the police; race and culture will dwell, no doubt, upon the supposed racism of the majority of the white population, and will reproduce the fashionable rhetoric of the anti-racist lobby.

What can be done about the widespread, and increasing, politicisation of the curriculum? In the first place, we should define exactly what is meant by 'political literacy', and having done that we should address ourselves to the question of whether it is desirable that children should be encouraged to develop it. If, and only if, the answer to that question is yes, might we consider the question of how best 'political literacy' might be cultivated. The present situation is so grave, precisely because none of those questions has been asked, and no real debate has been engaged in. Subjects are becoming politicised in a left-wing direction, aided and abetted by government and responsible educational institutions, with little appreciation of the damage which is being done.

The notion of 'political literacy' has so far been a conceptual tool lying solely in the hands of the radical. To be politically literate has meant little more than to follow progressive fads and fashions – anti-racism, anti-sexism, multiculturalism and nuclear disarmament – and to persuade oneself that oppression and exploitation exist within every area of 'capitalist' society. If, however, 'political literacy' were to be spelled out as involving a thorough grounding in political education – including a knowledge of the history and development of parliamentary democracy, the relationship between Church and State, the role of the monarchy, the processes of government, the nature of local government and the possibilities for democratic political participation – if political literacy involved the study of *those* issues, then it might contain some positive value, and might also go a long way towards developing those qualities of respect, tolerance and the sensitive appreciation of complex issues which the advocates of the GCSE system wish to see. Political education might then become one component amongst others within the curriculum, leaving other subjects free from political influence.

But it is clear that that idea of political literacy is not favoured by those who are responsible for devising the new politicised syllabuses. For it is clear that a child could possess political literacy in *that* sense, and not be left-wing. Indeed he could be politically literate while believing in national pride and patriotism, in the superiority of his own culture, in the necessity to defend it, even by means of a nuclear deterrent, in the value of capitalism and liberal institutions, in monarchy, property and the rule of law. But the appreciation of social, political, economic and environmental issues advocated in nearly every subject is promoted by radical and progressive educationists, for whom political literacy is inseparable from socialist and egalitarian values. This being the case we should strenuously resist the teaching of controversial issues in the classroom. For, despite the arguments of the sociologists, there *is* a difference between the values which grow naturally from induction into a culture and the proper acquisition of factual knowledge, and the deliberate, conscious fostering of political attitudes with the explicit aim of changing the world. A traditional British education did much to foster principles of respect and sensitivity, and to encourage an awareness and appreciation of people different from ourselves. It did these things, however, almost unconscious· ly and certainly delicately, by teaching children first to value their own society and heritage, and secondly to feel proud of themselves as part of it. Through literature, classics, scripture, history, geography and science, children were encouraged to develop gradually, to accumulate a store of knowledge, and to appreciate the richness of other cultures only after acquiring a genuine culture of their own. That we have moved far away from that atmosphere of real learning is evident from the language and exhortations which have introduced the GCSE. But if the result is 'progress', then one may be forgiven for thinking that progess is far from obviously desirable.

If some sense of balance is really to be maintained in school subjects it will not be enough merely to rely upon the integrity of individual teachers. Unfortunately, the process has gone too far for that to suffice. The government should draw up standards of good teaching practice, stating that teachers should refrain from expressing their own political views on topics which are controversial in nature. Where contentious issues have to be addressed, or where they arise naturally within the classroom, teachers should be required to present all sides of an argument and to use materials which properly reflect all alternative positions. It might be necessary to create an independent body whose function is to monitor teaching materials connected with controversial issues, and ensure that they are fair and unbiased.

As I mentioned earlier, there are several thousand Mode 3 courses running throughout the country. The fact that such courses are devised and assessed with the minimum of external control means that they are open to a greater degree of abuse. It might be worthwhile, therefore, if some greater degree of external control could be established, in order to ensure that balance is maintained.

Such measures will no doubt be extremely unpopular with radical teachers. But I believe that they would be welcomed by the majority of parents. A government which claims to be sensitive to the wishes of parents, and which has committed itself to enlarging the scope for parental involvement in the educational process, cannot remain blind to one of the most serious dangers facing education today. One can only hope that parents will involve themselves more closely in discussing the kind of education that they wish their children to receive, and that their concerns will be listened to sympathetically.

16+: AN ALTERNATIVE EXAMINATION

Nicholas Debenham

At the time of writing of this essay, pupils are preparing to take O-Levels, for the last time, in June and November 1987; and others are preparing to take GCSE papers, for the first time, in June 1988. The two courses are running side by side.

Although the coming of the GCSE was long heralded, and preceded by much committee work, issuing of National Criteria, and setting of syllabuses, it was not until late 1986, when specimen examination papers appeared, that the form of the new examination became clear. It is the contention of the writer, a headmaster of one of the smaller independent schools facing this new event, that key elements in education are being phased out, to the great loss of the whole education system and of the country; and that they ought to be immediately restored before they slip wholly from the teachers' memory. Hence the proposal of an 'alternative' examination at 16 years which, while not ignoring any useful new trends in education, would be strongly traditional in form.

The initial reaction of a number of independent school headteachers to the GCSE, once the drop in standards was apparent, was either to put pupils in for the new examination a year early, and spend the following year making good the gap between GCSE and the start of the A-level course; or to let them take the GCSE 'in their stride' while continuing to educate them along traditional lines. It is now becoming clear that these ideas are not practicable. The GCSE does not make great intellectual demands on pupils; but it does take a great deal of their time; and the subject-teachers, harassed by new syllabuses, new teaching methods and the demands of course-work, are dropping everything except what is explicitly required by the new examination. Nor is anyone anxious to prejudice pupils' chances by entering them early, especially if insufficiently prepared. It is already clear from past experience that the examination syllabus decides what is taught in schools; and what is not examined will, sooner or later, not be taught.

The GCSE is having far-reaching consequences. Even the preparatory-schools, which were already questioning their own curriculum and contemplating fundamental changes in their approach to examinations, are wondering if they should further adapt their teaching, at ages below 13, in line with the new thinking. At the other end of the system, A-Levels are being searchingly reviewed because, as is now acknowledged, the GCSE course will not, in all subjects, leave a pupil prepared to begin an A-Level course. Proposals will certainly be put forward, under cover of 'broadening' the A-Level course, to lower its standard; and a four-year degree course may be needed for pupils to obtain their qualification a year late.

It is here worth stating what, in the writer's view, is the natural educational development of a human-being. The early years, from 5 to 10, should be spent in learning the elements, beginning with reading, writing and arithmetic; and in learning by heart multiplication tables and the grammar of any languages they study. At this stage learning is easy and enjoyable. The child learns to work with care, and the result is both accurate and beautiful. He is not required, at this early stage, to think much.

In the next phase, from 10 to 16, the child's mental

capacity evolves and he learns to put his knowledge to use, by solving problems. The traditional subjects which most facilitate this process are arithmetic, where straight calculation is gradually adapted into problems which reveal its practical application; algebra, via equations, factorising, and the like; and geometry including the formal theorems and proofs based on Euclid. Classical languages also provide a ready-made mental discipline under which the child's knowledge of grammar is put to use in the translation of Latin (or Greek) into English and the composition of English into accurate and, eventually, artistic Latin. The introduction of the sciences, particularly physics and chemistry, strongly aids this process of mental development. In this same phase, education broadens to give necessary knowledge of the world, and of the achievements of man: thus, history and geography are introduced; economics and law, if time permits, could also be started; and as full an experience as is practicable should be offered to each child in the world of literature, music, art and drama.

During this phase, from 10 to 16, a balanced curriculum should be given to all, and no specialisation should be allowed, so that the child is as competent and experienced as his or her nature allows, in all the principal fields of learning. There should be no options. How can a child judge the long-term benefit of a subject? All he can see is the hard work. It is the option system that has killed the finest academic disciplines, and caused changes in all subjects designed to make them attractive to pupils – as if they were products to be sold.

However, in the next phase, from 16-18, there is a complete change. At 16, or thereabouts, the child enters the adult world and begins to be responsible for his own actions. It is no longer necessary, or possible, to continue education on a broad front. The young adult has to choose a subject, or subjects, which strongly engage his interest, and study those subjects in depth. Whatever it is he really wants to know about, that he studies. There is much talk nowadays about early specialisation. As has been stated above, specialisation before 16 is out of place; at 16 it is just right. For most of those who continue with education at this age, it will lead to a university degree and, insofar as is possible, mastery of a chosen subject.

This brief sketch has mentioned only the academic side of education. But it is to be hoped that, however, strong the academic demands upon children, their classroom education will be balanced by a full and vigorous programme of physical training on the one hand, and by spiritual and moral instruction on the other. These should continue throughout the period of full time education. Both are being sadly neglected by today's schools. In the end people will wake up to the fact that you cannot educate the mind, without also carefully training the body, and nurturing the spirit: not, that is, if you aim to turn out a whole human being.

But to return to the main theme: as the essays in this volume have tried to show, the GCSE involves, for all those pupils capable of taking O-Levels, a fundamental and serious lowering of standards. The idea of an alternative examination at 16 is an attractive one. It would retain the essential character of the O-Levels, and restore some traditional features which have already been lost. It would enable students to embark on A-Level courses without further preparation, and thus strengthen the case for leaving the A-Levels as they are. It should receive ready recognition from those university authorities who prefer to receive students who have been properly grounded in their subjects.

The alternative examination would aim, first and foremost, to produce students who know by heart the fundamental principles of their subjects and who can apply them; who can think, and reason; who can express themselves clearly and logically; who can write concise, correct English; who can relate a composition validly to a theme; and who are educated in at least the elements of a full range of traditional subjects. That is what universities want, and what employers want.

The alternative examination would be open to all. It is, of course, likely to appeal only to schools where the traditional English education is alive – in most cases, independent schools, but by no means only the large and well known ones. It has been called an elitist idea. In a sense, it is, It acknowledges the self-evident fact that only a small part of the population is capable of achieving academic distinction, and recognises that the country needs men and women who are properly educated to fill key posts in government, in the professions, in industry, in the universities, in the church and in the world of the arts. It is in no way the intention that such posts should be the preserve of the rich or the well-connected: but it is natural that they should fall to those who get the best education.

In the succeeding paragraphs of this essay, a list of subjects is given which, it is suggested, might form a 'core curriculum' for an alternative examination. Art, music, and craft of all kinds are omitted because, although they should certainly be practised by all, they may not need to be examined. Papers would be easy to set, because they could follow the lines of existing O-Level examinations, for which the syllabus, content, and method of assessment are already familiar to secondary teachers. Subjects here considered are as follows: scripture; classical languages; modern languages; English language; English literature; mathematics; physics; chemistry; biology; history; geography and law. A good student might take, perhaps, ten papers. Each subject is considered in turn, in order to establish its distinctive contribution to the overall development of the pupil.

(1) Scripture The title is deliberately chosen. Present trends in Religious Studies (as the subject is now called) favour a 'thematic' approach, in contrast to the O-Level, which was firmly based on the study of texts. In the GCSE, some study of texts remain, but it is subordinated to other aspects; and there is no longer the time or the incentive to study in detail, still less in depth. In the view of the writer, religion (as such) is not a proper study for examination: it is a matter of personal commitment; and as for studying someone else's religion, that is little short of impertinence. The proper study is of the great scriptures of the world; and in a Christian country the obvious priority is the study of the Gospels. There is no substitute for children studying for themselves, at first hand, the words and the life of Jesus Christ. Nor should this be confined to children of Christian families: experience shows that such study is greatly enriched by the contribution of children of other faiths. Time permitting, all could study (say) the Bhagavad-Gita as well as the Gospels, so that they could compare the words of Shri Krishna with those of Jesus. This would do far more to promote understanding between nations than the superficial and often tendentious studies of 'comparative religion' now being widely promulgated. There is a new crop of text books on Religious Studies, many of which grossly misrepresent the great traditions which they are supposed to illuminate. Even the best text book, in this subject, is dangerous. Children need direct contact with scripture, free from dubious interpretation and 'selective' quotation. They should read for themselves what Jesus said.

(2) Classical Languages The great educational tradition in this country is founded on the study of Latin and Greek. The procedure was: first, learn the grammar by heart; next, learn how to speak and construct the language by translation and composition; next, read and appreciate the great authors in the original; next, absorb, appreciate and value the literature, philosophy, art, history and thought of the classical age. Much of this scheme has been retained, in schools where Latin and Greek are taught, but the approach has been, as it were put into reverse: 'Classical Civilisation' (taught by text book) has grown rapidly in popularity as a subject for those pupils not thought capable of dealing with the language itself. Of those who actually tackle the language, most begin by reading Latin (or Greek) and appreciating its meaning as best they may. Composition, that is writing Latin or Greek sentences, prose, and verse, has almost disappeared; and so has most of the learning of grammar – all this since 1939, for reasons well-known and easily understood. But the result is that Latin and Greek no longer provide a good mental discipline.

The old way was the right way: learn the grammar while the pupil is still young (under 10) and loves learning; apply it in handling the language, and beginning to read the authors, from 10 to 16; read widely from 16 to 18, and develop fluency and style in composition, both written and oral.

An alternative examination would seek to restore grammar to its proper place, as the foundation of the learning of language, and would re-introduce straight grammatical questions into examination papers. It would also restore translation from English into Latin (or Greek), as well as the reverse process, and banish the 'comprehensions' which have been increasingly introduced as soft options. Composition, both in prose and in verse, would be retained, if only as an option.

(3) Modern Languages The aims in the teaching of modern languages (which is demonstrably made easier by being associated with the teaching of classics, but which must be capable of standing on its own feet) would be: to enable pupils to converse fluently in a foreign language, and to read and appreciate its literature; but at the same time to gain an understanding of how language (of all kinds) is constructed.

An examination would therefore contain grammatical questions, and candidates would be required to be able, in addition to translating French (etc.) into English, to write, and speak, grammatical and idiomatic French.

(4) English Language The O-Level examination has been reduced in scope, and now consists of 'comprehension' questions and 'essays'. The 'comprehension' element tests a candidate's ability to understand and appreciate written English, both prose and poetry, and his ability to answer a question. The 'essay' questions are a mixed bag: some require no more than an ability to write simple narrative. The examination is narrow in scope and gives little encouragement to those who wish to show they can write accurately, artistically or relevantly.

An alternative examination would require, from all candidates, a *real* essay: that is, a composition upon a set theme, allowing pupils to put both sides of a case and draw valid conclusions. This is an excellent test of mental capacity; indeed it might be said to be the supreme test of a person's education: can he comprehend some issue of importance, adduce facts and marshal arguments relevant to it, weigh them, and draw a valid conclusion? A lawyer, a priest, an academic, a politician or an industrialist, all need such ability, and they need to be trained when young. So this would be the most important feature of the examination.

It would also be necessary, given the present poor state of education, to test a candidate's ability to write *correct* English, where a good standard of handwriting, punctuation, grammar and vocabulary would be required. Unless this aspect is explicitly examined, it is unlikely to improve from its present abysmal level. Until recently, O-Levels contained examples of incorrect English which candidates were asked to identify and amend. These questions are a good test of acumen and should be restored.

Comprehension questions could also be retained. Précis might be included. Précis-writing, which involves deciding what to cut out of a passage without losing its essential features, is an exercise in judgement and aids lucid writing, free of unnecessary words.

(5) English Literature The present O-Level syllabus requires detailed study of set texts (normally two books). The examination includes compulsory questions upon extracts from the texts, not identified in advance, so the pupils have to know the book well, as well as essays upon themes related to the book as a whole. This admirable form of examination could be retained. The choice of books for study is of key importance, and if only two books are to be examined they should be chosen from among the few authors universally acknowledged to be masters of written English, so that pupils who study them are enriched and inspired by them.

English literature is a treasury: and, in particular, its poetry. One would like all English boys and girls to sample enough of it to acquire the taste for life. One would like all to study, in depth, at least one of Shakespeare's plays, so that they can appreciate for themselves the greatest writing the Western world has ever seen. For sheer depth of knowledge, insight into human nature, and limitless scope, Shakespeare has no rival. But Chaucer, and the dozen or so English poets of first rank, are well worth study: and experience suggests that if they are not studied at school they will not be studied at all.

In the alternative examination wide reading by pupils, outside the set texts, would be strongly encouraged, but not explicitly examined.

(6) Mathematics A number of interesting developments in the teaching of mathematics in recent years have combined to make the subject more attractive, and less barren, than it once was. This is welcome. In other respects, however, mathematics is no longer providing the mental discipline which children need as a foundation for their learning.

Firstly, the learning of multiplication tables by heart has been questioned then abandoned and then partly restored – but is still widely neglected. A senior HMI, specialising in independent schools, recently said that he thought there were 'better ways of spending time' than in learning tables. The coming of the pocket calculator has, of course, made it possible to give answers to mathematical questions without the learning of tables, and the early years of practice of mental calculation of all kinds – particularly when tested orally – is a most serious omission, comparable with the abandonment of the learning of Latin grammar. Of all subjects, mathematics most brightens the mind and pro-duces mental quickness and sharpness. Anyone who teaches young children orally with simple question-and-answer methods knows this: so does anyone who watches a bookie's clerk at a racecourse. Prodding the keyboard of a calculator does no such thing.

The advent of the calculator, particularly in the primary school, has been most harmful. To see a garage mechanic (as the writer once did) faced with a mechanical breakdown of the calculator in his petrol pump, deducing the cost of eight gallons by writing the price down eight times in column and then adding up, is painful.

Associated with the coming of the calculator is the view, widely expressed, that 'getting the answer right is not the most important thing'. This makes for slopping thinking and bad work. No one thinks much of an engineer who understands his subject but miscalculates the stresses on a bridge. Fortunately, many school teachers, essentially straightforward people, still use ticks and crosses. Anyone with eyes to see knows that children like getting things right, and take pride in not getting them wrong. Such an attitude should be fostered.

An alternative examination in mathematics would outlaw calculators altogether, and re-introduce problems of calculation which favour those with the acumen to spot short-cuts (such as 'cancelling'), those who could factorise at sight and those well-practised in mental mathematics. Also, the child would have to get the answer right to get any marks. Algebra is an excellent discipline, in which the pupil starts by obeying simple rules which, miraculously, yield the desired result: the solving of equations would be prominent in the examination, because it tests the pupil's insight and perseverance. Euclidean geometry, including formal proof, would also be restored. The result would not be unlike the O-Level as it was a few years ago.

(7) Physics, Chemistry and Biology These subjects, which are the principal strength of today's examination, are relatively well examined in the GCSE, mostly because the examiners, recognising the inevitable, have provided papers of different standards for pupils of differing ability. (This applies also to mathematics.)

An alternative examination, however, would seek to establish, first, that candidates knew the fundamental laws of science, could quote them accurately, and could apply them to problems both in a theoretical and a practical context. It would also insist on part, at least, of each paper being answers in good written English, in the belief that a scientist should not only understand his subject but be able to explain it in clear and accurate terms.

(8) History There has been a tendency in recent years to teach modern, i.e. twentieth century, history in preference to that of earlier periods, because it is thought to be more 'relevant' to the young people of today. Certainly it has allowed political bias to enter more freely, and has contributed to an increasingly pejorative view of Britain's role in the history of the world.

The aim of teaching history in British schools is, in the writer's view, a simple one. First, the children need an outline of historical events over a considerable period, preferably from the Roman conquest until today. Not only does this provide useful general knowledge, but also a framework of reference against which to judge the value of British institutions, such as the monarchy, parliament, the church, the law, the universities, the City of London, and so on. These cannot be understood without a historical perspective. Next, the children need to know of the glorious achievements of the past, and also the failures and mistakes, so that they may take pride in the nation's strengths and understand its weaknesses. They need to know (for instance) the character of the Anglo-Saxon race from its early beginnings: freedom-loving, law abiding, loyal to the king. They need to learn of the extinction of this freedom under the Normans and its gradual re-establishment, after long strife, by the Great Charter, by the principle of *Habeus Corpus*, by the development of the Common Law, and the calling of parliaments; of the endless struggle to teach the Stuart Kings that 'the King is under God, and the law: for the law makes the King'; of the catastrophic results of the needless, and illegal, execution of the king; of the establishment of a balance of power in the constitution between monarch, lords and commons; and of the slow but gradual shift towards democracy every since. They need to be told of Britain's achievements in keeping Europe free of tyranny: of Drake's defeat of the Armada; Marlborough's supremacy over the armies of Louis XIV; the crushing blows inflicted upon Napoleon by Wellington and Nelson; and of the overthrow of Hitler under Churchill. They need to see clearly the great forces ranged against each other in the world today; the strengths and weaknesses on both sides; and where right and justice may be found. This noblest of subjects must be tackled fittingly, so that pupils may value their inheritance and their country's great institutions, and acknowledge their duty to secure justice and freedom, so far as is possible, for all people.

An alternative examination would seek to establish that students were grounded in knowledge of facts and dates; that they understood the significance of the events they described and so far as possible, their causes; and that they were able to write fully, lucidly and without irrelevant additions. The skill *par excellence* of the history student is the ability to write an essay, in which he gives an accurate account of relevant historical events, relates them clearly to a theme, and draws a valid conclusion. The examination would consist principally of a number of essays of this kind.

(9) Geography Geography is a subject of high practical utility, and is founded partly upon the skill of drawing maps. This aspect has been played down by modern geographers, and the subject has been expanded up to, and across, the borders of several associated subjects, such as economics, sociology, statistics, and so on.

It would be useful to emphasise, and re-establish at its centre, not only map-reading, but the making of maps; to place so-called 'physical' geography, with some geology, next in importance; and to cover the 'human' aspects only when the earlier have been mastered.

Children ought to know the main features of the surface of the globe, and the names of oceans, seas, rivers, mountains and cities. The only tolerable way of learning them, which lifts the exercise into artistry, is by the creation of accurate and beautiful maps.

An alternative examination would be largely practical. Map-reading tests should be military-style, out of doors; and map-making skills should be tested, not only at the drawing board, but in the countryside. There is nothing better than making a map for getting children to understand one.

(10) Law Although law (and the British Constitution) is not much studied at secondary level, there is a good case for it. All young people should know about law. It is probably too much to expect them, at this stage, to study Blackstone's *Commentaries on the Laws of England* (as was done a hundred years ago) but there are excellent modern text books available.

An alternative examination would seek to establish that candidates know what law is; where its authority lies; who makes it; and the differing scope and jurisdiction of laws of different kinds – not excluding Jesus's famous quotation from Mosaic law, 'Thou shalt love thy neighbour as thyself'. They would know on what basis of law their own fundamental freedoms rested, and have an idea of how in practice the situation differed in other countries, and at other times. As in history and English, the main method of examining would be by essay.

Such, then, would be the core curriculum on which an alternative examination might be based. If the comments given above reflect the personal views of the writer – and no doubt they do – a syllabus for each subject could easily be agreed, provided there is the common aim of preserving traditional education intact.

It may be said that such a curriculum is out of touch with today's world. There is no truth in that assertion. Pupils are still being educated in this way, at good schools, and they do outstandingly well in all fields. More and more parents are coming to recognise the value of a traditional approach to education, and we should take steps to satisfy their demands for disciplined study and higher standards.

The important aspects of education do not change: the laws of the universe do not change; nor the laws of grammar; nor the laws of mathematics. Education should reflect this stability and resist the fads and fancies of the self-styled educational 'experts'. The pace of change in education should not be hasty, lest matters of great consequence should disappear altogether from men's minds, thus impoverishing their culture and undermining their nation's most important source of strength.

APPENDIX 1

Northern Examining Association, GCSE Integrated Humanities (for examination in 1988)

I The Community

The study of the community should provide the student with an understanding of the nature of the community in which he/she lives, the origins of that community, the extent to which individuals are able to exert an influence on the community, the constraints on personal involvement and on change. The study should also identify general concepts of communities, the identification of individuals with the community and problems associated with different types of communities.

1. The basis of the community

   (a) The sense of belonging to a community.

   (b) The nature of the community and its origin: associations with industry, agriculture, commerce, residential areas; links with the larger community.

   (c) The community as a development organism: growth, decline and impoverishment.

   (d) Interdependence of individuals and of groups of individuals.

2. Features of the community

   (a) Populations: size and structure and their changes.

   (b) Wealth and income, social class.

   (c) Housing.

(d) Communications: links within the immediate community and with the larger community.

(e) Land use.

3. Provision of community services

(a) Local and central government.

(b) Voluntary organisations.

(c) Religious organisations.

(d) Profit-making concerns.

4. Community action

(a) Formal and informal decision-making processes.

(b) Avenues for community action: pressure groups, individual action.

Centres are free to study the module by concentrating on, e.g. a community (or communities) in decline/growth/conflict.

II Law and Order

The study of law and order should provide the student with a basic understanding of the relationships between individual rights and responsibilities and legislation or *mores* designed to protect the values of the society. It is not intended that students should be concerned with the law *per se* or with a survey of the illustrations which comprise the English legal system. Students should appreciate the basis of the legal system, the principles on which it operates and the steps which our society takes to regulate the behaviour of the population.

1. Forms of regulation

(a) Rule-governed behaviour in the home, school, religious community and the wider society.

(b) The status and function of rules, conventions, *mores*, religious codes and laws.

(c) Law in complex societies; difference between civil and criminal law.

2. Rights and responsibilities

(a) The extent to which the law affects the individual's freedom of action.

(b) The varying age of responsibility.

(c) The individual and the state and the place of statutory bodies.

(d) Torts and covenants; landlords, tenants and neighbours.

(e) Conflict between minority group norms and the law.

3. Crime and the criminal

(a) The definition of a crime.

(b) Age-related patterns of criminal behaviour and the social context of juvenile delinquency.

(c) Social versus hereditary basis of criminality.

4. Law and justice

(a) Parliament as a law-making body and as a representative of the population.

(b) The police as a law-enforcement agency.

(c) The court system: the role of the jury, magistrate, judge and counsel in the interpretation of law and the dispensation of justice.

(d) Theories of punishment: corrective, deterrent, retributive and restorative.

Centres are free to develop an issue which involves the legal aspects and policing of a crisis or instance of civil unrest.

III People and work

The study of people and work should lead the student to a consideration of the concept of the necessity of work and for the sound development of the individual and of society. The study should provide an understanding of the main spheres of work, the nature of the work in each sphere and the factors which determine the conditions of work. The study should also foster an appreciation and understanding of the interdependence of workers.

1. The need for and the effects of industry and commerce

(a) Work to obtain a livelihood: the nature, extent and effects of unemployment.

(b) Other forms of work: unpaid work, voluntary work, work in the house, the 'black economy'

(c) Work to improve the wealth of the country: the relationship of prosperity and production, payments for imports with exports, maintenance of the balance of trade.

(d) The need for specialisation of work activities in an industrialised economy compared with work patterns involved in a subsistence economy.

2. Primary, manufacturing and service industries

(a) Economic, historical and geographical context of industry (locally and generally).

(b) The nature of the relationship between, and interdependence of, each stage of industry.

(c) Constraints on the choice of work: entry and qualifications, employment trends and opportunities, job satisfaction, the influence of the new technology.

3. The organisation of work

(a) Ownership: state, public, private.

(b) Management: types and functions, the role of the C.B.I.

(c) Workers' rights and responsibilities; the role of the trade unions and the T.U.C.

(d) Relationships in job situations: collective bargaining, dispute procedures, worker participation in ownership and management.

4. The government and work

(a) The distribution of work: relocation, development areas.

(b) The protection of work: subsidies and grants, import

controls

(c) The control of work: control of wages, prices and dividends; monopoly and competition, restrictive practices; taxation.

(d) The regulation of work: legislation concerning working conditions, product standards, fair trading, consumer protection.

(e) The role of the Manpower Services Commission in youth training.

IV The mass media

The study of the mass media should provide the student with an understanding of the history, ownership and influence of the newspapers, radio and television. Students should be able to make comparisons between media in the United Kingdom and similar ones in other countries. The interrelationships of the different media should be appreciated as well as the influence they exert upon one another.

1. The literary media

(a) A comparison between the following types of newspapers in terms of their ownership characteristics and the ways in which standards are controlled and maintained (editorial responsibility, Press Council): dailies/weeklies, local/national, 'popular/quality'.

(b) A study of magazines and comics in terms of their variety and competition for readership; specialist interests and social groups.

(c) A consideration of the extent to which books (fiction and non-fiction) exert a mass influence: availability, circulation, stimulus to other media.

2. Audio-visual media

(a) Radio: the structure of broadcasting, the functions and characteristics of the BBC/commercial radio networks, the establishment and maintenance of standards.

(b) Television: the functions and characteristics of television output (information and entertainment), competition between the BBC and commercial TV, local and national interests, viewing habits, the establishment and maintenance of standards, the implications of the development of cable and satellite television.

(c) Video: the development of this medium, the pursuit of audiences and the censorship of material.

(d) Cinema: the commercial nature of this industry, the pursuit of audiences and the censorship of material.

3. The influence of the media

(a) An understanding that the output of the media influences attitudes and behavioural patterns both as the result of deliberate attempts to establish attitudes or wants and as the result of imitative behaviour.

(b) Advertising through the media: its aims, techniques and importance as a revenue.

(c) Influence on leisure activities.

(d) Influence on attitudes.

(e) Influence on awareness.

(f) Influence on behaviour: imitative behaviour and the extent to which aspects of behaviour can be attributed to the influence of the media.

4. Control of the media

(a) Consideration of the extent to which the mass media in the United Kingdom is free from political control, making comparisons with examples from state-controlled media.

(b) Consideration of the potentiality of the media for propaganda and indoctrination.

(c) Consideration of the extent to which the mass media reflects or determines the nature of its audience, e.g. 'pop culture'.

V Consumer affairs

The study of consumer affairs should provide the student with an understanding of the rights and responsibilities of consumers and retailers, the function of organisations promoting their interests, the issues involved in a consumer society. The study should provide the student with the opportunity to consider the extent to which, in our society, the production of consumer goods is aimed at meeting the needs and wants of the members of society and the extent to which the members of society accept that what is produced is what they need and want. The student should consider such topics as 'built-in obsolescence', 'wastage', and 'the throw-away society'.

1. Shopping
    (a) Types of retailing: small traders, voluntary chains, super markets, etc.
    (b) Chain of production/distribution, from manufacturer to consumer.
    (c) Methods of buying/selling: hire-purchase, mail order, budget accounts, credit cards, cash, etc.
    (d) Prices: indices and reasons for variations in prices, special promotions, government influence on possible determination of retail prices.

2. Sales promotion
    (a) Market research.
    (b) Advertising: techniques of persuasion, 'hard sell', 'soft sell', etc.; use of different media (television, radio, press, hoarding, packaging); work of advertising agencies, ethics of advertising; codes of practice.
    (c) Selling methods: promotions, packaging, 'new' products.

2. Consumer protection

(a) Buyers' and sellers' rights.

(b) The work of government agencies, local and national.

(c) The consumer and the law: Trade Descriptions Act, Sale of Goods Act, Supply of Goods and Services Act, etc.

(d) The work of specialist organisations of a variety of types: Consumers' Association, British Standards Institute, Design Council, Citizens' Advice Bureau, National House Builders Registration Council, etc.

VI Education

The study of education should provide the student with an occasion for appraising his educational experiences and future opportunities, while appreciating the country's educational system as a whole in all its diversity. By focusing attention on general aims and principles, the organisation of schools, and approaches to learning, the study should give the student a deeper understanding of the many controversial issues in this field.

1. The purpose of education

(a) The responsibility of parents and the state for the development of the young.

(b) The curriculum: the concept of the curriculum as the whole educational experience, its aim, the criteria and the responsibility for determining the curriculum, e.g. multicultural, anti-racist, anti-sexist approaches.

(c) Subjects: the nature of subjects, the place of individual subjects within the curriculum, the degree of choice, the criteria for choice and current developments in subject integration and core curricular initiatives.

(d) Preparation for life: vocational aspects, 'educational' aspects; assessment and certification, the degree to which information on educational attainment is important for life chances.

2. The provision of education

(a) The state and private systems of compulsory schooling; the methods of allocating pupils to schools.

(b) Educational welfare services and school attendance.

3. Relationships within education

(a) Relationships between teaching and learning methods and student motivation, ability and academic grouping.

(b) Relationships between pupils; the social effects of school organisation, e.g. houses, streams, sets, etc.; the influence of peer groups.

(c) Relationships between teachers and parents: contacts between school and home, Parent-Teacher Associations and the teacher *in loco parentis*.

(d) Relationships between the school and the community which it serves: the neighbourhood school, governors, the local education authority.

4. The wider perspective

(a) The relationship between social class, educational opportunity and life chances.

(b) Education beyond compulsory schooling: further education; higher education; apprenticeships.

(c) Educational patterns in other countries.

(d) The problem of illiteracy.

VII The family

The study of the family should provide the student with an insight into the differences in family structures and how the family relates to society. It is expected that the student will consider the factors which influence the nature of family structure and role, both those influences tending to preserve an existing framework and those which promote change.

1. Family structures and functions

(a) The family as a unit for the raising of children and as an economic unit related to the degree of social and economic mobility required in the society.

(b) An outline of family structures: extended, nuclear, single-parent families, communes.

2. Relationships within the nuclear family

(a) Those that exist between parents: love, marriage, parental responsibility.

(b) Children: relationships with parents (discipline/ affection/dependence), duties within the family and relationships with other members of the family.

(c) Preparation of children for their future role as parents.

3. Relationships of the family with society

(a) The concept of childhood, adolescence and child rearing: the conventional nuclear family structure as one method of child rearing; alternative approaches related to different forms of social structure (relative absence of blood links and marital ties).

(b) Working parents and the changing status of women and men.

(c) The extent to which the state accepts responsibility for some of the functions of the family: benefits, education, support for single-parent families, children in care, care of the old and handicapped, etc.

(d) Adolescence and the conflict between intra and extra-family relationships, family responsibilities, dependence and the search for independence.

(e) The extent to which the family experience is relevant to the choice of marriage partner and the establishment of a new family unit.

VIII Persecution and prejudice

The study of persecution and prejudice should provide the student with some insight into the ubiquitous nature of the field of human behaviour on the personal, local, national and international levels. This theme is more concerned with the recognition of persecution and prejudice than with the prospects of changing attitudes, although it is expected that logical, reasoned arguments would weigh more than unsupported, one-sided opinions of whatever standpoint, in the assessment of students' work.

1. The universality of prejudice
    Xenophobia, segregation, scapegoatism, victimisation, ostracism, bigotry, endogamy, paranoia, stereotyping, snobbery, elitism, etc.
2. The techniques of persecution
    (a) Anti-location.
    (b) Avoidance.
    (c) Discrimination.
    (d) Physical attack.
    (e) Massacre/genocide.
Students should be expected to demonstrate an understanding of this sliding scale of persecution, in part or in total, and to appreciate how one step on it provides a threshold for the next.
3. The influence and determining effects of social, political and economic conditions.
4. The study of at least one major area of persecution or prejudiced behaviour at home or abroad
    (a) Race.
    (b) Politics.
    (c) Religion.

(d) Gender.
(e) Class.
(f) Physical handicap.

IX Inequality

The aim of this module is to involve the student in consideration of the unequal distribution of wealth and power throughout the world, causes and effects of this inequality and the range and implications of possible solutions. In particular, students should develop an awareness that the remedies to inequality adopted depend on the analysis of its causes.

1. Inequality based on class, race and gender
2. Inequality within nations
    (a) The problems and possibilities of measuring inequality in terms of income, wealth and power.
    (b) The causes of inequality: e.g. possession of wealth and power, control of resources, access to education.
    (c) The effects of inequality: e.g. on housing, health, diet, social welfare; the 'vicious circle' of cause and effect.
    (d) Possible solutions and palliatives; usefulness and limitations of Government intervention (legislation, taxation, welfare state etc.) assistance from charities; self-help; individual or community action; political and economic change; reform, revolution.
3. Inequality between nations
    (a) Problems and possibilities of measuring inequality in terms of GNP, natural resources, ownership of resources and wealth.
(This section may provide the opportunity for statistical work)
    (b) The causes of inequality: e.g. trading patterns, lack of capital, colonialism, external control of resources (e.g. by

multinational companies) and physical environment.

(c) The effects of inequality, e.g. starvation, famine, political unrest.

(d) Solutions and palliatives: the usefulness and limitations of Aid (loans/grants, tied/untied) from government, charities, banks, international organisation (IBRD etc.);

(e) reform of trading patterns e.g. GATT, Lome Convention, Brandt Commission reports etc.; self-help e.g. increasing agricultural productivity, nationalising foreign investments, import-substitution, producer cartels (e.g. OPEC).

4. Reactions to inequality

(a) Attitudes of rich to poor and of poor to rich in terms of individuals and nations.

(b) The extent to which extreme inequalities are irrevocable.

X War

The module is not concerned with the description of particular wars, their specific causes and events but rather with a consideration of war, actual or potential, as an ever-present reality. The student should consider the many forms which warfare might take, the justifications given for war (e.g. 'the just war') and for war-readiness as well as the means of preventing and controlling wars. The study should lead to a consideration of the place of war in present society and of whether there are better ways of solving world problems.

1. The roots of war

(a) Ideology.

(b) Political and economic advancement.

(c) Reaction to real or suspected threat; state of war-readiness.

(d) Honouring obligations e.g. agreements.

(e) To achieve self-government or to overthrow existing order.

(a) Ideological warfare: propaganda.

(b) Subversive warfare: secret services, coups.

(c) Economic warfare: boycott, blockade, tariffs.

(d) Guerilla warfare: terrorism, hijacking, urban warfare.

(e) Conventional military warfare: conscripts, volunteers, regulars, mercenaries; weapons.

(f) Potential future warfare: biological, chemical and nuclear warfare.

3. The effects of war

(a) The extent to which war succeeds in meeting its initial objectives.

(b) Effects on individuals: status of combatants and non-combatants.

(c) Developments resulting from war activities: scientific, technological, medical and social progress.

4. The portrayal of war

News, films, television, literature: the relationship between the presentation and intentions of the presenter.

5. The prevention and control of war

(a) Institutionalised means: Geneva Convention, treaties, UN.

(b) Popular movements: pacifists, conscientious objectors, CND, Humanists and religious attitudes.

(c) Disarmament negotiations.

(d) Neutrality.

XI Politics and government

The study of politics and government should provide students with an understanding of general political concepts, the decision-making process and the role and functioning of government. Students should be aware of the pervasive nature of politics: that political relationships exist wherever there is a relationship of power. Politics, thus, is not merely an activity dominated by governments or political parties but may involve individuals and small groups in a wide variety of situations. Students should understand the nature of political ideologies and their relationship to the institutional framework of politics at local, national and international levels. Students should be aware of the diverse nature of various political systems as well as that which operates in their own political environment. The study of contemporary local, national and international political issues should be encouraged in order to develop in pupils an understanding of differing political standpoints and the ability to discuss these issues in a reasoned manner.

1. Themes and general concepts

(a) Defining 'the political': the all-pervasive nature of politics, levels of political interaction, micro and macropolitical situations, the resolution of conflict.

(b) Political concepts: power, authority, coercion/consent; forms of power-persuasion, economic, physical coercion; types of authority–traditional, charismatic, legal/rational; legitimacy; the state; democracy and freedom–democracy as an ethical ideal, competing choice, majority/minority rule, equality, human rights; political culture–conflict/consensus, stability/instability, levels of political development, participation/non-participation, apathy; political sovereignty; the 'political spectrum'.

The themes and general concepts identified above may be expanded upon and given particular treatment in the coverage of the remainder of the topic.

2. Types of political systems

(a) Absolutism, monarchy, feudalism.

(b) Liberal democracy, capitalism.

(c) Socialism, communism.

(d) Fascism, tyranny, military dictatorship.

(e) Multi-party states, one-party states.

3. Parliamentary democracy

(a) Political constitution, Bill of Rights, universal suffrage, different voting systems, the Electoral Register.

(b) Separation of powers: executive, legislature, judiciary.

(c) Government and parliament: parliamentary scrutiny of government, 'strong' government/open government, the committee structure and the legislative process, select committees.

(d) Political parties and parliament: constituency interests, ideological influences, role of the party whips.

(e) Changing patterns of voting behaviour.

(f) The influence of the mass media and opinion polls.

4. The decision-making process

(a) Theories of power: pluralist/elitist.

(b) The power of the Prime Minister's office.

(c) Cabinet government and collective responsibility.

(d) The role of the Civil Service and the Judiciary.

(e) Civil Service/Ministerial relationship.

(f) Interest group access to government departments.

5. Areas of governmental responsibility with reference to party- political ideology

(a) Management of economic/industrial policy: laissez-faire, Keynesianism, monetarism, planning, mixed economy; public ownership/private ownership; full employment; inflation.

(b) Framework of central/local government: the exercise of power and the democratic principle; local government finance; the rate support grant; local rates levy, 'rate-capping'; councillor/officer relationships.

(c) The international perspective: foreign policy and

foreign aid; the diplomatic service, United Nations; European Economic Community; role of I.M.F., World Bank, etc.

(d) The coercive apparatus of government: the police–accountability, impartiality, operation control; the the civil power, the influence of NATO, defence policy.

XII Pollution and conservation

The study of pollution and conservation should help the student to develop an interest in, and a responsible attitude to, our natural environment. It is not intended to be part of an environmental studies course but one which provides students with an understanding of the moral, social and political implications of the use/abuse of the environment. Students should be able to make comparisons between the respect for the environment shown by some cultures and its exploitation by others. They should be aware of the attempts made to confront the issues posed by environmental pollution and conservation and also the potential responses to the problems which these issues give rise to.

1. The ecological balance

(a) The balance of nature and how it can be disturbed or maintained.

(b) Ecological problems.

2. Resources

The political, social and moral issues in the following: the nature and distribution of the world's resources; trade in resources; the utilisation of resources by the rich North and the poor South; waste of resources; the role of colonialism and neo-colonialism in the use of world resources.

3. Pollution

The political, social and moral background to, and implications of, pollution.

(a) The implications of the rapid growth of pollution.

(b) Despoilation of the natural environment (land/air/water) resulting from the effects of waste and/or misuse of resources.

(c) Pollution caused by advanced technology.

(d) Land abuse: dereliction, urban sprawl, the effects of agriculture, desertification, refuse disposal.

4. Conservation

(a) Examples of conservation measures: international, efforts.

(b) Endangered species and plans for their conservation.

(c) Animal rights.

5. Alternatives

(a) Alternative technologies and energy sources: intermediate and appropriate technology as an alternative to advanced resource-intensive technology.

(b) Alternative lifestyles: theories and practice; self-sufficiency.

(c) Recycling of natural resources.

XIII Beliefs

The study of beliefs should provide the student with an understanding of the various conceptual approaches to the topic. Students should understand how beliefs are formed. They should also be aware of the wide range of moral, religious and political beliefs which exist within societies and the ways in which beliefs can affect social behaviour and social change. Students should be aware of the inter-related character of beliefs. Thus, a moral belief may simultaneously have religious and political effects.

1. Definition and formation of beliefs

(a) Defining a belief and understanding the key terms: opinion, myth, faith, agnosticism, dogma and ideology.

(b) The cultural transmission and maintenance of beliefs via social institutions such as the family, education, religious sects and denominations, peer groups, the mass media, political organisations, etc.

(c) The various types and complexity of beliefs: moral, religious and political.

(d) The basis and relative validity of beliefs: what makes one belief more cogent than others? Are values relative or absolute?

2. Moral beliefs

(a) What makes a belief moral, immoral, or amoral?

(b) The relationship between morals and social behaviour.

(c) The potential conflict/consensus between the moral beliefs of individuals and those of social groups, communities, societies, nations.

(d) Cultural and historical approaches to morality.

(e) The nature of the moral/social beliefs and values involved in the following: the 'permissive society', youth cultures and sub-cultures, war/peace, conservation/pollution, abortion, euthanasia and vivisection.

3. Religious beliefs

(a) The study of religions, denominations and sects: either a comparative survey or a study in depth.

(b) Religion in the UK: identification of the various groups and an analysis of their membership in terms of numbers, sex, age, social class, etc; moves towards the secular society.

(c) Religious beliefs concerning creation, death, fate, after- life.

(d) The significance of religious ceremonies e.g. initiations, baptism, confirmation, marriage, etc.

(e) The institutional structure of religious organisations.

4. Political beliefs

(a) The relationship between political beliefs and forms of economic organisation.

(b) Pre-democratic political beliefs.

(c) The democratic principle.

(d) Varieties of political beliefs.

(e) The political beliefs of contemporary social movements.

XIV Health

The study of health should provide the students with a greater awareness of the need for a healthy society and environment. It should also provide an understanding of the provision of a climate for the discussion of topics of a controversial nature which involve the Humanities and health issues and which lend themselves to individual research. Students should be encouraged to look at problems and solutions available to society in general on health issues as they affect the quality of our life. The study should aid greater understanding of the responsibilities involved in the development of a healthy body, healthy mind and healthy society.

1. Personal Health Body Management and Human Biology

(a) Adaptation to environment e.g. physical and mental stress.

(b) Exercise: the need for and after effects of local amenities.

(c) Health habits and personal hygiene.

(d) Effects on the body of alcohol, drugs and tobacco.

(e) Common infectious diseases, including sexually transmitted infections.

2. Food Selection

(a) Nutritional needs of the body.

(b) Nutrition and health, e.g. slimming, obesity, stress and anxiety etc.

(c) Eating patterns of individuals and the community.

(d) Multicultural society and varying diets.

3. Relationships

(a) Parents and adult-authority (i.e. schools, services at work etc.)

(b) Peers.

(c) Emotional and social development, effects and relationships.

(d) Sexual relationships: other and same sex.

(e) Marriages and/or other long term relationships.

(f) Learning to cope with loss and separation.

(g) With the mentally ill and physically handicapped.

(h) As situations for smoking, alcohol and drug activities.

4. Parenthood

(a) Family roles and structures.

(b) Separation and divorce and its effects upon children.

(c) Fostering, care responsibility.

5. Community Health

(a) The National Health Service and private health schemes.

(b) Roles of, and relationships with, doctors and hospital staff.

(c) National and community health issues such as contraception, abortion, immunisation, fluorides etc.

(d) Attitudes to physical and mental illness and handicap.

(e) Role of voluntary organisations and clinics etc. e.g. Marriage Guidance Councils, Samaritans, Brook Advisory Clinics, Alcoholics Anonymous etc.

6. The environment in which we live

(a) Meeting the needs of the community, for living space, leisure and mobility.

(b) The effect of the environment on physical and mental

health.
7. Safety
   (a) Road traffic education and driver education etc.
   (b) Safety at Home.
   (c) School and work; Safety at Work Acts.

XV Leisure

The study of leisure time should make the student aware of the balance which has developed historically between the amount of personal time spent in work activities and that allocated to leisure pursuits. The study should provide an understanding of how leisure patterns have developed, the nature of leisure activities and the factors determining the criteria within which leisure patterns have been created. The study should also allow students to view their present and future potential leisure patterns with a high priority given the likelihood of the increase in the amount of time which will be available for these pursuits in the future.
1. The historical and geographical development of leisure activities
   (a) Social class and status related to leisure pursuits e.g. The Grand Tour, Spa resorts etc.
   (b) Holiday resort development: the growth of holiday resorts from the 18th century to the present day.
   (c) The changes in holiday activities and their effects on resorts: land use, facilities etc.
   (d) The influence of the railways, the car and the aeroplane.
2. How do people spend their leisure time?
   (a) A comparison between the leisure activities and the sociology of leisure of different generations.
   (b) The growth of 'time for leisure'.
   (c) Leisure: its constructive and destructive uses: active

and passive leisure; financial constraints on leisure patterns; the leisure patterns of the employed, the unemployed and the retired.

(d) Local leisure facilities and their national counterparts e.g. tennis centres, ice-rinks.

(e) A comparison between the UK and its EEC counterparts with regard to leisure.

(f) Education for increased leisure time.

3. The concept of the holiday

(a) The influence of the media on holiday activities.

(b) Holidays at home and abroad: the growth of tourism abroad; package holidays; sample studies of specific areas e.g. Costa Brava, France.

(c) Family and group holidays.

(d) The use of the countryside as a leisure facility: National Parks – conflicts of interest, further development in the future.

APPENDIX 2
A Guide to the GCSE

The following information may be of use to parents and those others who would like to find out further details concerning the GCSE examination. Explanations of some terms and phrases which may be unfamiliar are also given.

The General Certificate of Secondary Education (GCSE) has been designed as a single examination system designed to replace the dual system of GCE and CSE examinations. Teaching for the GCSE began in September 1986 and the first pupils to sit the examinations will do so in the summer of 1988.

The new system is being administered by six Examining Groups, each of which coordinates the administration and syllabus design of a number of Examination Boards. The Groups and the Boards which fall under them are as follows:

LONDON AND EAST ANGLIAN GROUP (LEAG)
East Anglian Examinations Board, The Lindens, Lexden Road, Colchester CO3 3RL (Tel: 0206-549595).

London Regional Examining Board, Lyon House, 104 Wandsworth High Street, London SW18 4LF (Tel: 01-870-2144).

University of London School Examinations Board, Stewart House, 32 Russell Square, London WC1B 5DP (Tel: 01-636-8000).

MIDLAND EXAMINING GROUP (MEG)
East Midlands Regional Examinations Board, Robins Wood House, Robins Wood Road, Aspley, Nottingham NG8 3NR (Tel: 0602-296021).

Oxford and Cambridge Schools Examinations Board, 10 Trumpington Street, Cambridge CB2 1QB (Tel: 0223-64326).

Oxford and Cambridge Schools Examinations Board, Elsfield Way, Oxford OX2 8EP (Tel: 0865-54421).

Southern Universities Joint Board, Cotham Road, Cotham, Bristol BS6 6DD (Tel: 0272-736042).

The West Midlands Examinations Board, Norfolk House, Smallbrook Queensway, Birmingham B5 4NJ (Tel: 021-643-2081).

University of Cambridge Local Examinations Syndicate, Syndicate Buildings, 1 Hills Road, Cambridge CB1 2EU (Tel: 0223-61111).

NORTHERN EXAMINING ASSOCIATION (NEA)
Associated Lancashire Schools Examining Board, 12 Harter Street, Manchester M1 6HL (Tel: 061-228-0084).

Joint Matriculation Board, Manchester M15 6EU (Tel: 061-273-2565).

Northern Regional Examinations Board, Wheatfield Road, Westerhope, Newcastle Upon Tyne NE5 5JZ (Tel: 091-286-2711).

North West Regional Examinations Board, Orbit House, Albert Street, Eccles, Manchester M30 0WL (Tel: 061-788-9521).

Yorkshire and Humberside Regional Examinations Board, 31-33 Springfield Avenue, Harrogate, North Yorkshire HG1 2HW (Tel: 0423-66991).

Yorkshire and Humberside Regional Examinations Board, Scarsdale House, 136 Derbyshire Lane, Sheffield S8 8SE (Tel: 0742-557436).

NORTHERN IRELAND SCHOOLS EXAMINATIONS BOARD (NISEC)
Northern Ireland Schools Examinations Council, Beechill House, 42 Beechill Road, Belfast BT8 4RS (Tel: 0232-704666).

SOUTHERN EXAMINING GROUP (SEG)
Associated Examining Board, Stag Hill House, Guildford, Surrey GU2 5XJ (Tel: 0483-506506).

South East Regional Examinations Board, 2-10 Mount Ephraim Road, Tunbridge Wells, Kent TN1 1EU (Tel: 0892-35311/2/3/4).

Southern Regional Examination Board, Avondale House, 33 Carlton Crescent, Southampton SO9 4YL (Tel: 0703-32312).

The South Western Examinations Board, 23-29 Marsh Street, Bristol BS1 4BP (Tel: 0272-273434).

University of Oxford Delegacy of Local Examinations, Ewert Place, Banbury Road, Summertown, Oxford OX2 7BZ (Tel: 0865-54291).

WELSH JOINT EDUCATION COMMITTEE (WJEC)
Welsh Joint Education Committee, 245 Western Avenue, Cardiff CF5 2YX (Tel: 0222-561231).

All the syllabuses which are produced by the Examinations Board are monitored and approved by the Secondary Examinations Council (SEC).

AIMS AND CRITERIA

The general aims of the GCSE are stated in *GCSE: a General Introduction* which was published by Her Majesty's Stationery Office in 1985.

The GCSE National and Subject-Specific Criteria were produced jointly by the Department of Education and Science (DES) and the Welsh Office. They were published by Her Majesty's Stationery Office, and are available from P.O. Box 276, London SW8 5DT (Tel: 01-622-3316) and from all major bookshops.

Subject-Specific Criteria are available for the following

subjects: Art and Design; Biology; Business Studies; Chemistry; Classical Subjects; Computer Studies; Craft, Design and Technology; Economics; English; French; Geography; History; Home Economics; Mathematics; Music; Physics; Religious Studies; Science; Social Science; and Welsh.

In addition, Subject Guides in each of these subjects have been produced by the SEC and the Open University. Each guide explores the subject criteria and recommended course content in detail. The SEC also produces two Working Papers on the assessment procedures for the GCSE: Working Paper 1: *Differentiated Assessment in GCSE* and Working Paper 2: *Coursework Assessment in GCSE*.

THE GRADING SYSTEM

There are seven grades awarded for the GCSE: A, B, C, D, E, F, G. A, B and C will have standards equivalent to GCE O-Level grades A, B and C.

D, E, F and G will have standards at least as high as CSE grades 2, 3, 4 and 5.

The Subject-Specific Criteria all contain descriptions of the abilities and skills which candidates should be able to demonstrate in order to achieve grades C and F.

MODES 1, 2 AND 3

Mode 1 examinations are administered by the Examining Group on the syllabuses they have set. Written examinations are assessed by external examiners. Coursework assessments are carried out by the pupils' own teachers.

Mode 2 examinations are administered by the Examining Group but the syllabuses are devised by individual schools. Assessments are carried out as in Mode 1 examinations.

Mode 3 examinations are set and marked by individual schools but are 'moderated' by an Examining Group. Moderation is the process whereby standards between different examinations are aligned. There are two forms of moderation: moderation by inspection, in which candidates' work is inspected and original assessment adjusted to bring them into line with general standards; and moderation by consensus in which groups of teachers consider the work of each other's candidates.

READING

Further information concerning the GCSE and how it operates can be found in a book written by Maureen Mobley et al., called *All About GCSE*, published by Heinemann Educational Books in 1986. In addition, Macmillan publishers produce a series of books on different subjects, which try to help pupils to prepare themselves for the new courses and examinations. These books are available in the following subjects: English; Mathematics; History; Geography; Biology; Physics; Chemistry; French and German; Social Science; and Economics.

NOTES

Chapter 1: English

1. *English GCSE: A Guide for Teachers*, Secondary Examinations Council, p.14.
2. *ibid.*, p.12.
3. *ibid.*, p.19.
4. *ibid.*, p.24.
5. *ibid.*, pp.27-28.
6. Frank Whitehead, 'The Present State of English Teaching' in *The Use of English*, Volume 28, no.1, September 1976, p.14.
7. *English GCSE: A Guide for Teachers*, *op cit.*, p.6.
8. *ibid.*, p.9.
9. *ibid.*, p.9.
10. Prof. John Carey, 'We Are What We Know'.
11. *ibid.*
12. Thomas Hardy, *The Return of the Native*, Macmillan, p.276.
13. *English GCSE: A Guide for Teachers*, *op cit.*, p.30.
14. Frank Palmer, 'English: Reducing Learning to Short-Cut "Skills"' in *The Wayward Curriculum*, 1986, Social Affairs Unit, p.49.
15. University of Cambridge Local Examinations Syndicate Report on A-Level Paper 800/3, Chaucer and Other Major Authors, Summer 1977, p.1.
16. *English GCSE: A Guide for Teachers*, *op cit.*, p.21.
17. Frank Palmer, 'Optional Discipline' in *The Salisbury Review*, Volume 4, no. 4, July 1986, p.19.

18. *English GCSE: A Guide for Teachers*, op cit., p.11.
19. Dr Robert Burchfield, 'The Disappearance of Grammar' in *The Times Educational Supplement*, 28th November 1986; Anthony Burgess, 'Don't leave it to the KGB to rescue the English Language' in *The Daily Mail*, 17th July 1986.

Chapter 2: History

1. A. Marwick, *The Nature of History*, Macmillan, p.240.
2. Nick Williams in *Teaching History*, Historical Association, No. 46, p.12.
3. S.F. Lang, 'The Sacred Cow History Project' *TES*, 11th March 1986.
4. Welsh Joint Education Committee Syllabus History (A-Modular), Aim No 1.2.
5. Welsh JEC, Specimen Question Papers to above, p.24.

Chapter 3: Mathematics

1. J. Bruner, *The Process of Education*, 1978, Harvard University Press.
2. R. Skemp, *The Psychology of Learning Mathematics*, 1979, Penguin.
3. LEAG, *Underway with GCSE Mathematics*.
4. G. Frege, *The Foundations of Arithmetic*, 1950, Oxford University Press.
5. Z. Isaacson, *Teaching GCSE Mathematics*, 1987, Hodder and Stoughton.
6. HMSO, *Mathematics Counts*, 1982, (The Cockroft Report).

Chapter 5: Music

1. *Music GCSE: A Guide for teachers* (Secondary Examinations Council in collaboration with The Open University), p.8.
2. Hamish Preston, Contribution to *The Times Educational Supplement*, 14th March 1986.
3. *Music GCSE: A Guide for teachers, op cit.*, p.22.
4. *ibid.*, p.27.
5. *ibid.*, p.29.
6. *ibid.*, p.27.
7. *ibid.*, p.25.
8. *ibid.*, p.13.
9. *ibid.*, p.23.
10. *ibid.*, p.19.
11. *ibid.*, p.30.
12. *ibid.*, p.42.
13. *ibid.*, p.26.

Chapter 6: The GCSE Philosophy of Education

1. This paper is based on a study of the National Criteria for the GCSE, as laid down by the DES, and of the Teachers' Guides to the various subjects issued by the Secondary Examinations Council (the body overseeing the GCSE) in conjunction with the Open University, and of the SEC's *A Guide to the GCSE*, published jointly with the BBC.
2. From 'The Present State of English Teaching' in *The Use of English*, Vol.28, No.1, 1976, p.14.

Chapter 7: Multicultural Education

1. I shall use the term 'multicultural' because of its wide currency, even though 'multiethnic' might be more accurate. For advocates of multicultural education are rarely concerned with white sub-cultures or with the cultural differences to be found within any given ethnic minority. Incidentally, I am acutely and embarrassingly aware of indulging in the vague and unexamined terminology which infects discussion of these matters. But to have engaged in critical examination of terms like 'culture' and 'prejudice' would have required a much longer paper; while to have avoided them would have required complicated alternative locutions.

2. HMSO, 1985, para.206.

3. HMSO, 1985, p.4.

4. HMSO, 1985, p.2.

5. HMSO, 1985, p.1.

6. *Education For All: Report of the Committee of Inquiry into the Education of Children from Ethnic Minority Groups.* HMSO, 1985, p.333, & p.769.

7. *ibid.*, p.475, p.424, & p.775.

8. 'National Criteria' for *English*, HMSO, 1985, p.5.

9. *op.cit.*, p.317f.

10. That African philosophy should be compulsory for all children is proposed by Madan Sarup, *The Politics of Multi-Racial Education*, Routledge & Kegan Paul, 1986, p.117.

11. *op.cit.*, para.204.

12. Quoted in the Swann Report, *op.cit.*, p.240.

13. *ibid.*

14. *op.cit.*, p.318.

15. See, for example, the peculiarly extreme proposals made in Madan Sarup's book, note 10 above.

16. 'A paradox of multicultural societies', *Journal of Philosophy of Education*, *16*, *2*, 1982, p.231-2.
17. See, for example, A.G.N. Flew, 'Three Concepts of Racism', *The Salisbury Review*, *5*, *1*, 1986; and Roger Scruton, 'The myth of cultural relativism', in F. Palmer (ed.), *Anti-Racism: An Assault on Education and Value*, Sherwood Press, 1986.
18. John Marks, 'The New Model Labour Party in Action', *The Salisbury Review*, *5*, *2*, 1987, p.27-8.
19. 'Post modernist bourgeois liberalism', in R. Hollinger (ed.), *Hermeneutics and Praxis*, Notre Dame 1985, pp.217-8. The author he quotes is Michael Sandler.
20. See J. Gundara, 'Education for a multicultural society', in J. Gundara, C. Jones & K. Kimberley (eds.), *Racism, Diversity and Education*, Hodder & Stoughton, 1986, p.11.
21. See A.G.N. Flew, *op.cit.*
22. 'A brief guide to the main issues of the Report', HMSO 1985, p.12.
23. The point I make in this paragraph is well-argued, in more detail, by Frank Palmer, 'Moral understanding and the Ethics of Indignation', in F. Palmer (ed.), *Anti-Racism: An Assault on Education and Value*, *op.cit.*
24. Quoted, with apparent approval, in the Swann Report, *op.cit.*, p.380, my italics.

Chapter 9: The Politicisation of Education

1. Michael Haralambos, *Sociology: Themes and Perspectives*, 1980 University Tutorial Press, p.185.
2. Brian Salter and Ted Tapper, 'Department of Education and Science: Steering a New Course', in Tim Horton (ed.), *GCSE: Examining the New System*, 1987, Harper and Row.
3. DES/Welsh Office, *GCSE: The National Criteria* 1985, General Criteria, Part 2, B, 19(i).

4. *ibid.*, Part 2, B, 19(k).
5. Roger Scruton, Angela Ellis-Jones and Dennis O'Keeffe, *Education and Indoctrination*, 1985, Sherwood Press Ltd.
6. *ibid.*, p.26.
7. Keith Orrell, 'Geography', in Tim Horton (ed.), *GCSE: Examining the New System*, *op.cit.*, p.85.
8. DES Criteria for Geography, Guidelines for content.
9. In N. Graves et al., *Geography in Education Now*, 1982, Institute of Education, London University. Quoted in Keith Orrell, 'Geography', *op.cit.*, p.92.
10. Robin Richardson, 'Culture and Justice: Key Concepts in World Studies and Multicultural Education', in David Hicks and Charles Townley, *Teaching World Studies*, 1982, Longman.
11. A fuller examination of the indoctrinatory nature of World Studies is presented by Roger Scruton in his pamphlet, *World Studies: Education or Indoctrination*, 1985, Institute of European Defence and Stategic Studies.
12. Christian Education Movement, Topic Folder number 3: 'Our World'.
13. David Selby, 'World Studies: Towards a Global Perspective in the School Curriculum', 1984, Association for the Teaching of the Social Science, 'Briefings', number 37.
14. Keith Orrell, 'Geography', *op.cit.*, p.95.
15. Sir Keith Joseph, 'Geography in the School Curriculum', speech to the Geographical Association, 19th June 1985.

INDEX